SHADOWS + REFLECTIONS
The Irish National War Memorial Gardens

Shadows + Reflections

THE IRISH NATIONAL WAR MEMORIAL GARDENS at ISLANDBRIDGE

ANNIE DIBBLE + ANGELA ROLFE

GANDON EDITIONS KINSALE

SHADOWS + REFLECTIONS
A photographic portrait of the Irish National
War Memorial Gardens at Islandbridge
with observations in poetry and prose

Published by Gandon Editions, Kinsale

ISBN 978-1-910140-32-1

Conceived and compiled by Annie Dibble
and Angela Rolfe; edited by Elaine Sisson

Design   John O'Regan (© Gandon, 2021)
Production   Nicola Dearey
Printing   W&G Baird, Belfast
Distribution   Gandon Distribution
                 and its overseas agents

GANDON EDITIONS
Oysterhaven, Kinsale, Co Cork, Ireland
tel +353 (0)21 477 0830
e-mail <gandoneditions@gmail.com>
instagram @gandoneditions
website www.gandon-editions.com
This is the 407th book on Irish art + architecture
produced by Gandon Editions. For information on other
Gandon books, see our catalogue or visit our website.

The funding of this book under the
Decade of Centenaries Programme
is gratefully acknowledged.

**An Roinn Turasóireachta, Cultúir,
Ealaíon, Gaeltachta, Spóirt agus Meán**
Department of Tourism, Culture,
Arts, Gaeltacht, Sport and Media

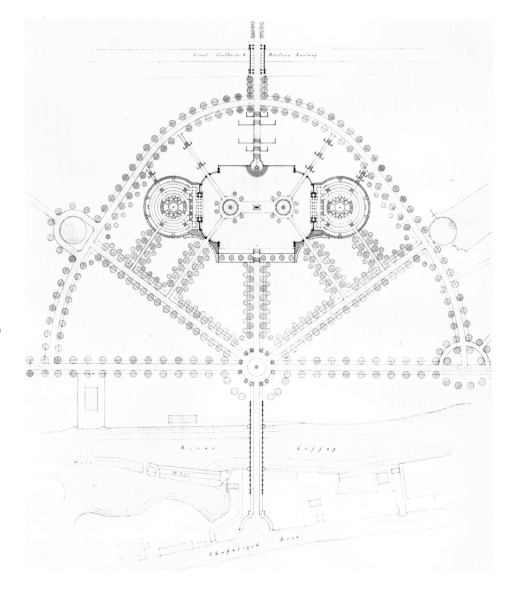

cover – *Obelisk, sunrise* • *June*

back cover – *Wisteria* • *June*

frontispiece – *Book rooms, sunset* • *July*

above
Irish National War Memorial – site plan
by Office of Public Works, 1931
(courtesy Irish Architectural Archive / TJ Byrne Collection)

Contents

Book rooms • July

An Act of Remembering

MICHAEL D. HIGGINS, President of Ireland

In *Shadows + Reflections*, the photographs illustrate with a stark beauty various elements of the eight hectares of lands on the southern banks of the River Liffey that comprise the Irish National War Memorial Gardens in Islandbridge. Beyond that beauty, this important interdisciplinary work, perhaps more poignantly, also offers an intriguing set of reflections drawn from the local, the national, the personal, the past and the architectural. *Shadows + Reflections* represents a meditation on war and lives lost too soon, on war's devastating personal and social consequences, and its immortalisation through memory and myth. The book redresses acts of exclusion in the act of remembering by privileging the experience that war constituted for women and the work of women during war.

Almost 50,000 Irish men and boys died fighting in the British Army during the First World War out of over 300,000 Irishmen who served, and the name of every fallen soldier is contained in the sumptuously illustrated Harry Clarke manuscripts in the granite book rooms within the Gardens. The youngest slain was only 14 years old: Thomas Woodgate from Callan, Co Kilkenny, drowned when *RMS Leinster*, a mailboat on its way to Holyhead, was sunk by a German torpedo off the Kish lighthouse in October 1918.

The Gardens were intended to be a memorial to all Irishmen who died in battle during World War I, but would go on to include those Irish who perished subsequently during World War II. The grand design of gifted architect Sir Edwin Lutyens was employed, and ex-servicemen north and south of the island (half were former World War I ex-British Army, and half ex-Irish Army) constructed the gardens. The skill and craftsmanship of the local stonemasons is evident in the finely carved stonework.

As the Gardens were laid out at a time not long after Ireland became partitioned, they became a reminder that, within Ireland, a profound divergence had occurred, with a majority lending its support to the struggle for independence, and its allegiance to the Free State that had emerged. A minority on the island had fought to preserve what it could of the former union with Britain, most of whom now found themselves within the newly formed Northern Ireland. In the South, the commemoration of those who fought and died in the calamity that was the First World War became embroiled in the project of nation-building and the emergence from British rule. As Annie Dibble points out in her essay in this book, 'for some, the monument [Memorial Gardens] became a symbol of all that was not right, not unified,… a folly, a witness to a nation's grief that would not be healed by buildings and ceremonial ritual.'

It is perhaps only in recent times, as the wounds of wars and conflicts – fought by Irishmen and women both on this island and further afield – have started to heal, that the Gardens have begun to be appreciated for their intrinsic beauty and have taken on a new resonance. In this important Decade of Centenaries in which we now find ourselves, as we mark and reflect on the formative moments and events from our past that constitute the sources of our contemporary Ireland, it is perhaps timely and, indeed, highly appropriate to explore the meaning and the symbolism of this particular and unique place that became the focal point for the annual Armistice Day commemorations in Ireland.

The decision to include only women's perspectives in this book was a deliberate attempt by the editors, Annie Dibble and Angela Rolfe, to rectify how women's voices have been largely absent from the history of the Gardens, and indeed how women's role in the wars of the early decades of the last century, including Ireland's independence struggle, was, for far too long, suppressed, concealed and ignored by the dominant historiographical narrative. So many women were left bereft as mothers, wives, sisters and friends following the carnage of the wars that the Gardens formally commemorate.

The seasonal nature of the setting depicted in the photographs included in the collection not only illustrates the Gardens' stark beauty and splendour, but also mirrors the changing use of the Gardens over time. This offers an escape from the prescribed meaning of the original project as a commemoration of the war dead into something more expansive, inclusive and perhaps even joyful in its remembering of the seasonal renewal of life. These images circumvent words, communicating that which verbal language cannot. As Annie Dibble puts it, 'Among the stone structures there is a constant movement of the elements that define our natural world; the weather, time and the seasons come together like fugitive troubadours around the architectural forms, pointing us to the fragile transience of life.'

Although commemorations of the dead by relatives of those Irish who served in the British Army had taken place at the site for a few years in the late 1940s and 1950s, an opposition, nationally dominant ideology – understandable but, perhaps, narrow – averse to Ireland's role in World War I, and critical of those who had volunteered to fight in World War II, prevented the Gardens from being formally opened and dedicated. The Gardens were subject to two Irish Republican paramilitary attacks: on Christmas night, 1956, a bomb was placed at the base of its Stone of Remembrance memorial cross and detonated, but the Co Wicklow-quarried granite withstood the blast with little damage, while another attempt was made to bring it down with a bomb detonation in October 1958, which once again failed, resulting in superficial damage. A subsequent lack of financing from the Government to provide for its upkeep allowed the site to fall into dilapidation and suffer acts of vandalism over the decades.

Since the 1980s, however, thanks to economic and cultural shifts occurring in Ireland, a regeneration programme commenced to tackle urban decay in Dublin. This included the tentative beginning of a change in the public's view of remembering Irish engagement in the World Wars, which led to a project of restoration work to renew the Gardens to their former splendour being undertaken by the Office of Public Works, co-funded by the National War

Memorial Committee. On 10th September 1988 the fully re-stored Gardens were reopened to the public, half a century after their creation. This was effectively the Garden's official opening, as the original unveiling, planned for 30th July 1939, never occurred owing to the looming threat of war.

I believe it would be a mistake to view the Gardens singularly as a symbol of posthumous glorification. Indeed, glorification of the gratuitous disregard for human life that the First World War, after all, represented would be morally objectionable. However, it is important to remember, recall and learn from the assumptions that led to the empires of Europe being so willing to lay waste to a generation of the young, including so many of their own sons and daughters, but also including those driven by poverty, insecurity, and those too that they sought to conscript from the publics of their colonial possessions. It is in all their diversity also important to remember those Irish men and women who died and the circumstances that led them to their deaths, as well as the broken lives that they left behind.

Today, the Gardens can encourage all of our citizens to engage with history and commemoration in a way that is inclusive, ethical, pluralist and honest, acknowledging the realities of our past, the rich tapestry that comprises the history of our island and its peoples. National monuments such as this are an important part of this process, and may assist in a deeper understanding and can assist in healing.

We must also acknowledge – and the history of these Gardens attest to this – that temporal proximity to certain events, or indeed the vagaries of contemporary national or world events, sometimes do not allow for a fully reflective commemoration, or one that captures the complexity of the circumstances that led protagonists to act in the ways that they did. Sometimes the ramifications of the events being commemorated have not sufficiently played out to allow for public reflection that can be sufficiently divorced from current political interest.

Ironically, a looming and, perhaps again, avoidable war in 1939, made the dedication of these Gardens at that time impractical. The Gardens themselves became, or perhaps were already, politically connected, with the IRA's border campaign of the 1950s and the later Troubles thus complicating the commemoration of those who had fought for the British Army, no matter what their backgrounds or their motivations were.

In the eyes of some, official Ireland has, at times, fallen short in its duty of public remembering in some significant areas of our shared history, perhaps most acutely the State's public acknowledgement of grief for those who died during World War I and those who died and suffered in the succeeding conflicts of the War of Independence and the Civil War. While there are reasons for this, it is nevertheless painful to think of all of those survivors, their families and the families and friends of those who died, who were left without an opportunity or symbolic location for public expression of their loss, of their grief and of their pain.

An approach to official remembering, in which the State was often absent or selective, resulted in grief layered on top of grief for many relatives of those who died, owing to the sense that they had not received due recognition for their loss. Redressing this exclusion does not involve any evasion as to the sources of war, the responsibility of those who saw it as part of their imperialism, nor does it involve any suggestion of moral equivalence in such sources of war. Honouring those lost to war is an acknowledgement of their humanity and of those whom they left behind.

The land on which the Gardens were created in the 1930s was originally occupied by foreign settlers to these shores almost 1,200 years ago – Vikings who had left behind them a treasure trove of artefacts that were unearthed alongside their skeletal remains when stones were quarried on the site to build the Great Southern and Western Railway line in 1850. This reminds us of the migratory nature of humans since the earliest times, and how we Irish continue to our present day to embrace the migratory experience in all its richness and for a variety of reasons.

Perhaps more importantly though, it also reminds us of our shared interconnectedness and frailty as humans. In our recollection of the dead from the two brutal world wars of the 20th century, we remember not only how, but why, they died. We remember the hubris of power, the arrogance, and dereliction of humanity in that power that conspired against them while they lived and led them to their deaths. We also remember the pain that was caused by the absence of official commemoration, by the amnesia that was affected by the State when it came to these dead, and the anguish that this caused to those they left behind. We mourn them and the opportunities quenched by their deaths, and we remember the pain of those they left behind. The Ireland of those decades had that pain, together with the impact of the 1918 pandemic and the anticipation of conflict that might have been avoided, to suffer.

The National War Memorial Gardens remind us of these difficult matters and encourage us to face up to complex aspects of our past. The wonderful photographs and insightful essays contained in *Shadows + Reflections* help us to transact that history as we seek to engage with our past through a process of ethical recall that strives to nurture memory and remembrance as a solid basis for a shared, inclusive future.

MICHAEL D. HIGGINS
Uachtarán na hÉireann / President of Ireland
July 2021

Memorial lawn • January

Book rooms • June

Introduction

ELAINE SISSON

Shadows and Reflections was first prompted by Annie Dibble's images of the Irish National War Memorial Gardens. Annie has been photographing the Memorial Gardens for over twelve years, noting the seasonal changes in light and landscape with an artist's eye. Collaborating with Angela Rolfe, that loose informal project has materialised into this book. The Memorial Gardens are nestled beside the Liffey, the main entrance tucked in behind Gael Scoil Inse Chór and St John of God School in Islandbridge. Designed by the English architect Sir Edwin Lutyens (1869-1944), the idea for a commemorative World War memorial for Irishmen was first proposed in 1919. However, it was not until 1929 that the present site, Longmeadows, was granted to the project, and the architecture of the Memorial Gardens that we see today was built in the 1930s. Yet Longmeadows has an older history: it is also the site of a Viking settlement and burial ground, so the symbolic significance of the Gardens is complex and layered.

Both Annie and Angela grew up in England, familiar with the pastoral landscapes invoked by Lutyens' style of architecture. By chance, both of them settled in Dublin, raising their families and making their homes close to the Gardens. Talking to them, they both acknowledged that the remembrance of war is embedded in their upbringings – childhoods marked by Armistice Day services, local monuments to the fallen dead, family histories and genealogies. The architecture and social infrastructure of commemoration and the legacy of war was woven into everyday life. It wasn't until coming to Ireland that they realised how contested this history was, how the politics of commemoration itself was conflicted. This tension was also evident in the attitudes of some local people towards the War Memorial Gardens, or 'Legion Park', associating it with imperialism, and unable, or unwilling, to see beyond given political or cultural frames. In some ways, both women think their backgrounds enabled them to recognise the architectural significance of Lutyens' memorial while at the same time compelling them to understand its complicated cultural meaning within an Irish context.

We live in different times now, where the role and sacrifice of Irish soldiers in World Wars I and II is acknowledged and properly commemorated. The Good Friday Agreement has ushered in a new climate of respect that has been truly transformational in our country. While the War Memorial Gardens host annual solemn services to remember the past, the Gardens are no longer just a site to honour the dead, but on sunny days are filled with families and dog-walkers, people sitting by the riverside watching the rowers from the boat clubs work their way to and from Chapelizod. Today, the Irish National War Memorial Gardens are variously referred to as the Memorial Park, the Gardens, the Rose Gardens, as well as the War Memorial Gardens. Indeed, the contributors to this book all refer to the site in these different ways. Lockdown has forced local, newer inhabitants to explore their neighbourhood, and it's possible the grounds have never been so well used as in the past year.

Over the years, as she photographed the Gardens, Annie noticed this transformation. Their changing use suggested an escape from the proscribed meaning of the original project as a commemoration of the war dead into something more expansive and more joyful. Annie's photographs bring the splendour of the gardens – – their grandeur, symmetry, mutability – centre stage. Her images are more than pictorial representations; they bypass words, communicating something verbal language cannot. In winter, the Gardens appear ghostly and dreamlike, centurion trees skeletal and bare. In others she has captured, to use Theodore Roethke's words, 'light making its own silence',[1] revealing the landscape at the cusp of becoming, framed at the turn of day or season.

The written contributions in *Shadows and Reflections* are companion pieces to Annie's photographic narrative. The idea to build a book around her images arose from conversations with people who share her interest in the place, among them poets, historians, folklorists, architects and artists who feel a connection to the Gardens. All of the contributors are female – a deliberate decision. The absence of female voices in the history and making of

the Irish War Memorial Gardens was notable, even though women were involved in the war and from the beginning were engaged in the plans to build a memorial. The aftermath of war is felt by everybody, yet, historically, the inclusion of women's experiences and thoughts has not been foregrounded. More recently, the Decade of Commemorations has reinstated the voices of women, and the result has been a fuller understanding of the past and of our own history.

'A garden', observed Emily Lawless, the Irish poet and naturalist, 'is a world in miniature and, like the world, has a claim to be represented by many minds, surveying it from many sides.'[2] The Memorial Gardens is a place that invites a rich variety of experiences, descriptions and meanings, and this is reflected in the contributions here. Annie Dibble outlines more fully her own response to the Gardens and the seeds of this project, while Angela Rolfe gives us a thorough and comprehensive overview of Lutyens' designs, and the planning and completion of the architecture of the Memorial. The Gardens are a site of memory, where we gather to remember the war dead, but they are also a reminder of the power of forgetting. Designed and built during a time when Ireland was extricating itself from an oppressive past, commemorating Irish soldiers' participation in the allied forces of World War I became a matter of forgetting rather than remembering. Gale Scanlan's and Angela Rolfe's contributions both outline the urgency and intention to remember. Gale's piece, in particular, highlights the physical labour and human endeavour involved in hauling, building and constructing the Memorial. The collective will that oversaw the design, planning and building of the Memorial is testament to the need to remember. The insistence on remembering, even when forgetting was easier, remains an important part of the sustainability of the Peace Process.

The Memorial Gardens are slowly revealed: as you enter them from whichever gate, you cannot see them all at once. As Angela Rolfe explains, this gradual revelation is part of the design, planned to create a particular experience. Standing in the open, flat heart of Lutyens' grass arena, where the War Stone occupies centre stage between two fountains, we become aware of standing between earth and sky, and the encircling architecture –the book rooms, the pergolas, and the symmetry of the rose gardens – invites the expansion not only of our vista but also of our feelings.

Many of the contributors explore, in poetry or memoir, the importance of the Memorial Gardens as a place for contemplation and for the imagination. There is a connection between internal self-cultivation, digging back through memories, and the Gardens as a created landscape involving maps, plans, surveys and designs. Ruth Johnson examines the archaeological history of the park, detailing how excavations in the 1930s revealed the older history of the land as a Viking burial ground. Ruth's contribution adds additional significance to the location as a site for commemorating the dead, and this connection is made in Anne Tannam's poem, 'Safe Shall Be My Going'. In a different kind of digging, Nuala Hayes uses the backdrop of the Gardens to filter through memories of her own family, of external events, of her links to the neighbourhood and community, of mutability, and of time passing.

Family connections to the First World War are explored by Rita Duffy and Fionnuala Waldron who, respectively, write movingly about a grand-uncle and a grandfather. Sheila O'Gorman gives us an idea of what soldiers might have experienced, the conditions of battle, and the terrible psychological toll that men carried home with them, if they managed to come home at all. The power of the Memorial and its gardens to evoke affective states – moods of melancholy, of regret, and of loss – are beautifully captured in poems by Jean O'Brien, Annemarie Ní Churreáin and Maeve O'Sullivan.

The designing, making and appreciation of gardens has been of importance to men and women since the days of ancient Persia and China. Literature is dotted with references to the pleasures and delights of gardens, from Andrew Marvell's evocation of 'a green thought in a green shade'[3] to Francis Bacon's declaration that a garden contains 'the purest of human pleasures'.[4] A garden symbolises something about the relationship between humans and the world embodying our complex relationship with the natural world. Long literary and philosophical traditions have celebrated the garden as a place of enlightenment, of moral repose, of tranquillity and restoration.

We find the same across religious traditions that acknowledge the garden as a poetic space particularly suited to introspection and the interior life. The metaphor of the garden as a place of spiritual reflection is an ancient one as it represents renewal, cycles of life, sun, earth, death, burial and resurrection. The Bible is abundant with allegories of toiling, sowing and reaping. From Eden to Gethsemane, the garden and gardening are central metaphors; when Mary Magdalene sees Christ at the empty tomb she initially mistakes him for a gardener. In Buddhism, gardens provide moral and intellectual restoration and enable us to cultivate an understanding of the world and the nature of reality: gardeners tend, they do not grow.

Gardens require continual attention, cultivation and labour to thrive, as do we. The ancient Greeks had a word for it, *eudaimonic*, meaning flourishing, or living in accordance with the best of human principles and endeavours. The idea of the garden as a space that brings out the best in us is particularly apposite when we think about the Irish National War Memorial Gardens, built to remember the price of our inhumanity, our capacity for conflict and brutality. These Gardens are a testament to the deeply scarring trauma of war at the same time as they mark our capacity for forgiveness, reconciliation, poetry and love.

──────

[1] Theodore Roethke, 'The Rose', *The Collected Poems of Theodore Roethke* (Doubleday Anchor, New York, 1975), p.198.
[2] Emily Lawless, *A Garden Diary, 1899-1900* (Methuen, London, 1900), p.14.
[3] Andrew Marvell, 'The Garden' (1681), in Elizabeth Story Donno (ed.), *Andrew Marvell, The Complete Poems* (Penguin, London, 2005), p.100.
[4] Francis Bacon, 'Of Gardens' (1625), (Hackett & Rickets, London, 1902), p.16.

Temple • March

Poplars • January, May

18

Poplars • June, November

Pergola • August

20

Where Two Architects Meet

ANNIE DIBBLE

The idea for this book arose from conversations with women who share my abiding love of the Irish National War Memorial Gardens. It is our local park, a magical, inspirational place. Years ago, in my early wonderings, it was not unusual to have it entirely to myself. In 2008 I began to bring my camera with me, and over time the captured images quietly developed a narrative of their own. I started to keep a weather eye and, on occasion, would awake at dawn, a gap in the perimeter fence giving early morning access before the south gate was opened: it was important to see and hear how the Gardens responded to daybreak when I was the only curious visitor.

Locally known as the Memorial Park, these Gardens are remarkable, conceived and created by a Memorial Committee who came together in 1919 out of a need to honour the young Irish men killed fighting in the First World War. Andrew J Jameson, chairman of Jameson's Whiskey Distillers and Memorial Committee Treasurer, engaged Edwin Lutyens as designer – an inspired choice. Lutyens was a visionary, and the Gardens are now considered to be one of the most outstanding war memorials in Europe.

It is well documented that at least 49,435 Irish men and boys died fighting for the British army during the Great War. The youngest was only fourteen years: Thomas Woodgate from Callan, Co Kilkenny, drowned when RMS Leinster, a mailboat on its way to Holyhead, was sunk by a German torpedo off the Kish lighthouse in October 1918. Imbued, in some cases, with a spirit of adventure, and eager to make a contribution to family income, it was not unusual for boys to lie about their age and enlist, but Woodgate's entry route was legitimate, having joined the RAF as an apprentice only a month prior to the tragedy.

The Gardens were intended to be a memorial to all Irishmen who died in World War I (and, later, World War II) and were built by ex-servicemen from both north and south of the recently formed Irish border. Some of them had together fought a common foe at Gallipoli, Passchendaele and the Somme. The book rooms were created to hold the eight volumes of names of those who died in the battles of 1914-18. However, the Gardens also served for some as a reminder that during the same period, Ireland had become irrevocably divided in its own struggle for independence. For many, the monument was a symbol of all that was not right, not unified, not sacred; the Memorial stood as a folly, a witness to a nation's grief that would not be healed by buildings and ceremonial ritual. Thus, once built, the Gardens were all but ignored by the local population for a long period of time.

Today, with time and maturation, with the movement of nature and the seasons, with the distancing from the wars they commemorate, it seems to me there is emerging a different story, one that is transcendent and still evolving. We can find beauty in the sudden flash of sunlight on stone or in a shadow cast at dawn on a midsummer solstice, the reflections on pond water in a July sunset, the movement of mist curling upriver on a March morning, the sound of rooks in the beeches at dusk, a lapwing skating on ice or a dog revelling in the fountain on a hot day. Because of the setting, the sky above is vast, the horizon low; the monuments can fill the line of vision, or they can be diminished by the enormity of the heavens.

I feel curiously drawn to the work of Edwin Lutyens. We were born ten miles and eighty years apart, in Surrey, England, and although I didn't know it at the time, I was introduced to his world when I was six years old. One of my friends lived in a house designed by him, and each Monday after school her mother took us into the stove-warmed kitchen and fed us hot buttered scones and sweet milk before our weekly ballet class. My childhood summer holidays were enjoyed playing on a beach in sight of Lindisfarne Castle, built high on a rock on a tidal island off the Northumbrian coast, whose 16th-century chambers Lutyens had refurbished.

For the last forty years I've lived in Dublin, just three minutes' walk from the Irish National War Memorial Gardens. When I moved first to Inchicore in 1980, the Memorial Gardens were badly run down. The granite structures, book rooms and sunken gardens were neglected, the stone was grimy (it was before the advent of smokeless fuel), and the wooden trellises of the pergolas were rotting. The grounds were wild and unkempt; horses roamed freely and a salmon pool at the river brought heron, seals and otters to forage for food.

For the Gardens this neglect was a bonus. The good-humoured wardens had a dedicated office and a pair of dogs, and I recollect them enjoying most of their waking hours walking with their animals and minding the park. They also could answer any question on its history and design. When their office was destroyed by fire, they were given a small wooden shed just below the hollies on the north terrace, where they drank tea and sheltered on rainy days. At that time the plantation was still young; underneath the many varieties of cherry trees grew a wildflower meadow. Each May saw an abundance of buttercups, ox-eye daisies, ragged robin and pink campion cavorting among the long grasses. Early spring on the slopes above the lawns boasted a carpet of cowslips dotted with orchids, but when the park was restored and the grass regularly mown, they struggled to bloom. Happily, the recent experiment with wilding is allowing them to return in abundance.

Along the riverbank and in areas that are still wild, you can find mugwort, figwort, hogwort, yarrow, horseradish, and a beautiful blue chickory that is becoming braver each year as it extends itself into a protected area above the water. Nearby, at the top of an elderly lime tree, is an increasingly robust mistletoe that has finally reseeded itself in some lower branches but not yet adopted any neighbouring trees. From August through to October, a large assortment of brambles provides successive crops of blackberries for pies and jams, their ample branches reaching over pathways, calling to be harvested.

In the river itself are all kinds of lily and yellow flag, giant king cups, dragonflies and damselflies, and on a sultry summer evening the sharpest eye will glimpse water bats skimming the surface for flies. All year round the river is home to seagulls, mallards, moorhens, cormorants, blue-billed diving ducks and herons. In the springtime, otters still play under the arches of Sarah Bridge, and around the weir every year swans raise their young, nesting under a willow. Alongside the hooded crows and jackdaws there is a growing colony of song thrushes, while blue jays nest in a nearby copse. Canada geese in their thousands make use of Liffey Gaels GAA playing field, just outside the boundary fence, on their way to or from Africa, and one early morning in June I came across a pair of mandarin ducks pottering about inside the entrance to Trinity Boat Club.

Lutyens insisted the granite structures were simply a setting for the herbaceous borders and majestic trees. In this, his final project, a professional partnership with English garden designer Gertrude Jekyll had run full circle: one of Jekyll's mentors had been an Irish-born landscape gardener, William Robinson. After working at Curraghmore House in Co Waterford, Robinson spent some time at Kew Gardens, before developing a style of planting quaintly called 'the English cottage garden', a synthesis of indigenous species and apparently random yet distinctive combinations of planting to create bold and colourful flower borders. In her later years, Jekyll continued to advise Lutyens and provide planting plans from afar, and although she was no longer alive when the Gardens were laid, she and Lutyens had created a legacy which saw its culmination in these herbaceous borders and pergolas. Here the flowerbeds come into their own in the spring and autumn against a backdrop of formal yew hedging, leaving the roses to bloom without excessive competition during the summer months.

Trees were considered and arranged in formal plantations which were overseen, in Lutyens' absence, by AF Pearson, keeper of the Phoenix Park. Pearson had trialled alternative planting arrange-

ments but inevitably returned to Lutyens' original plan. The smaller trees are organised in pairs and threesomes – pink hawthorn, holly, whitebeam and aspen. Once upon a time the area below the north terrace boasted avenues of Cornish elms, but they succumbed to Dutch elm disease so were replaced with limes which share their heady perfume in early summer. When my daughter was young, I often gathered the linden flowers to make a potion for her blonde curls. The elms that lined the diagonal avenues have been replaced by poplars – soldiers on guard duty – and as the year progresses their leaves move through shades of pale green and gold, until they finally fall to the ground and the path becomes a yellow river.

For years the keepers of these secret gardens opened the south gates at daybreak, and closed them at sundown, welcoming all-comers from Inchicore, Kilmainham, Islandbridge, Ballyfermot and Chapelizod for as long as the sun was up. I say 'secret' because at that time, most extraordinarily, apart from the locals and those rowers who sculled on the river at dawn, very few people knew of the park's existence.

But an open door can have a negative side, and, on one occasion, joyriders drove in at night and tore around the avenues before crashing into a stone column, causing the car to burst into flames, setting the wooden trellis on fire and knocking down the pillar. Happily, this stirred the authorities into action: the Trustees of the Memorial Gardens enjoined with the Office of Public Works to restore the Gardens to their intended glory. The restoration ran into a few stumbling blocks at first. Not all of Lutyens' plans had been completed, in part because of the lack of funds and a newly built Chapelizod bypass running roughshod over the southern perimeter of the Gardens, preventing completion of Lutyens' design for a grand entrance there. In the original drawings, the main gates were intended for Inchicore Road, flanked by a gate lodge on either side. The entrance along Memorial Road was to lead across an ornate stone bridge over the Dublin-Cork railway line via an avenue linking with the Horseshoe Road above the cross.

Lutyens' original plans for the Gardens included a temple, which, in cross-section, took the shape of a seven-pointed star, which was to have a curvilinear roof made of copper. Also planned was a stone bridge spanning the Liffey, giving pedestrian access to the Magazine Fort in the Phoenix Park as well as an entrance from the north side into the Memorial Gardens. But in 1995, when the OPW reviewed those plans, the Taoiseach of the day dismissed the idea of providing additional funding for direct access to the Park – for why, he said, would the people of Inchicore want to go there? So the bridges weren't built, but the temple was, bearing a domed roof different to the original plan, and an inscription of lines from the English war poet, Rupert Brooke:

> We have found safety with all things undying,
> The winds, and morning, tears of men and mirth,
> The deep night, and birds singing, and clouds flying,
> And sleep, and freedom, and the autumnal earth.
> – from 'Safety', 1914

Lutyens' distinctive wooden park seats were installed, although later removed and replaced with metal versions that are less prone to vandalism. The sunken gardens were replanted with 4,000 roses, filling the flowerbeds around the central ponds. Shortly after planting, many disappeared, only to turn up for sale in a van outside a local church one Sunday morning. The grass in the central lawn had been kept short by stray horses until a fence was erected that confined them to the high ground beside the bypass.

In more recent years, the Memorial Gardens have provided a stage on which to play out its own military dramas – annual remembrance services on 11th November and the second Saturday in July. Since its restoration it has welcomed visiting dignitaries, including Queen Elizabeth II and Mary McAleese, President of Ireland, in 2011, a visit that prompted a great frenzy of stone cleaning; for a while after, the granite was eerily white, dazzling in the sunlight. The park has also hosted the Trinity Regatta and has been the final stop for the annual Liffey Descent. The Francis

Ledwidge Society has held its annual meeting there, but, in all these, the focus for public throughfare has mainly been on the activities rather than the Gardens themselves.

Sir Edwin Lutyens died in 1944, and while he had been able to see the almost-completed monuments, the trees were only saplings. Today the copper beeches, Blue Atlas cedars, oaks and limes provide a setting of monumental proportion, just as he had intended. Because of the setting of the buildings, light plays a crucial role in the mood of the place, and in the same way as the beauty of a wilderness is described by changes in the weather, so it is here. I do sometimes wonder, though, if Lutyens reckoned with the reflection of the moon in the still water of the fountains, or imagined how they would respond to a mighty gale, or if he saw the way in which the evening sky might turn the stone to pink or white according to the weather, and envisage how the place might become almost ethereal in the ebb and flow of November mists or January snowstorms. And what about the drama of sunsets, or black thunderclouds? Are the shadows thrown at dawn or dusk across the sunken gardens accidental passengers? Had he imagined what birdlife would be generated, the autumnal fairy rings, the randomness of footprints on frost-white grass, or the trees throwing their skeletal winter shadow shapes over the flat, green lawns?

My visits became a meditation. As I passed time in the silence and solitude, it seemed to me that another dimension was present, the spirit of the place was telling its own story. It began to get under my skin. The time of day, the time of year and the position of the sun or the colour of the sky influenced my perception of the park. Each tree has its own character, and its own family of spirits. The senescent hawthorns in the meadow boast lichens on their ancient branches, indicating that the air is still reassuringly clean. The felling of a tree is a cause for deep grief: an elderly weeping willow, a limb lost during a storm, has a sapling planted at its base that will in time replace it. For now, they resemble a mother bent protectively over her child.

Among the stone structures there is a constant movement of the elements that define our natural world; the weather, time and the seasons come together like fugitive troubadours around the architectural forms, pointing us to the fragile transience of life. The genius of Lutyens and this play of nature become not one but two architects, creating a *kenos taphos*, a sacred space, for bodies who lie elsewhere.

The photographs themselves are markers in time, observations of a place that has developed a narrative that increasingly has the appearance of giving and sustaining life, reaching into something otherworldly, which is by its very nature ephemeral. With the fullness of time, the Memorial Park reveals a portal to another world, an encounter with the realm of the spirit.

In 2020, when everything changed and the world was suddenly overwhelmed by a great pandemic, people were startled back into their homes for months on end, emerging only to exercise and run essential errands. Ironically, the Memorial Gardens now offered a refuge from a new and fearsome plague, it offered a place where friends and families could meet at a safe distance, walk their dogs, feed the ducks, sit in the sun and picnic while they sheltered from an invisible enemy. It has finally become a place of and for the people.

At a time when the beauty of the earth and humanity is once again pockmarked with the devastating consequences of disease, famine and war, the unpopulated images in this book reflect another era and other conflicts. I have invited women who live locally and share my love of the Gardens to give their responses, through personal narratives and perspectives, contemplating its origins and reflecting upon its meaning.

——

A note about the photographs

In our habitual way of going about the day, the tendency to leap from percept to concept is extremely swift, and at the point when something is recognised or 'known' to us and given a name or position to fit with our realm of experience, we have usually stopped looking. We rarely get to truly see with all the senses open. In fact, when we are too familiar with something, we will create a story about it as if it belongs to another time or place; we become blind to what it is now, at this moment.

I've deliberately avoided detailed captions: a name doesn't change what is in our sightlines, but it can alter our perception and prevent our really seeing what is in front of our eyes.

I never get tired of visiting the Memorial Gardens. Every visit is a novel experience and I hope that these all-weather, all-seasons images will convey something of its magic to the viewer.

Sunrise • June

Solstice

ANNIE DIBBLE

Twilight stirs

the spirits of the night

into the pre-dawn air;

their congregation dispatched

amongst great coppered beeches.

As first light strikes pink granite,

a clatter of birdsong echoes

around the stones;

shadows, razor sharp

slice the morning air.

A glorious symphony

where two architects meet

to define the summer solstice.

Fountain • March

Fountain • September

War stone • November

Remembering Frank Waldron

FIONNUALA WALDRON

On 14th July 2016, along with members of my family, I laid a wreath at the Stone of Remembrance in the Memorial Gardens to mark the centenary of the death of our granduncle, Francis (Frank) Waldron, at the Battle of the Somme. The previous October, I had visited the site where he was killed, on the outskirts of Bazentin-le-Petit, a small village in the département of the Somme, set in rolling countryside. The windmill where he died has long gone, its absence from the landscape itself an embodiment of Frank's loss – shadowy, intangible and elusive. Barely 19, he had little time to make an imprint on this world. I was largely unaware of Frank's existence until well into adulthood, at least in part due to my own lack of attention to family stories; neither did I know much about his siblings, including my grandfather, his brother Thomas, who died in 1955, when I was two years old.

Now, Frank is present, particularly in his final year, through the memoir of his friend and comrade, Anthony Brennan, which my brother, Justin, located in the archives of the Imperial War Museum, having read about him in Myles Dungan's book, *They Shall Not Grow Old: Irish Soldiers and the Great War*.[1] He is still a fragile presence in the memories of his niece, Aileen Byrne, who remembers him described as 'a grand young lad' and 'always reading'.

Frank was born in Maudlin Street, Kilkenny, on 6th October 1896, the seventh child of Thomas Waldron, a railway porter, and Anne Waldron (née Dowling), who were married in Kilkenny city in 1881. By 1911 Frank also had a younger sister, Christina (Chrissie), born when Anne was 42. His oldest brother, John, aged 28, was a labourer, Patrick, aged 26, was a builder's clerk, and William (Bill), aged 24, was a carpenter. A year later, Bill would move to Longford to work as a joiner for a Mr Coote, building contractor. He signed up in 1915, joining the Irish Guards. By 1911, Thomas, my grandfather, was no longer living in the family home. Six years older than Francis, he married Anne Moore, my grandmother, on 27th November 1916.

At the age of 18, Francis left Kilkenny with his friend, Anthony Brennan, to travel by train to Richmond Barracks, Inchicore, where they joined the 2nd Battalion of the Royal Irish Regiment. Most likely, they were accompanied by others who enlisted around the same time, one of whom, Richard (Dick) Breen, a close friend, features regularly in Brennan's memoirs,[2] and George Buckley, described by Anthony as his 'best pal' after Frank. On the day the group of friends left Richmond Barracks for France, 27th July 1915, Brennan records that the shop windows near O'Connell Bridge were lined with young female shop assistants and the streets were thronged with well-wishers. Brennan recalls the friends as feeling 'very proud and heroic' and 'fully conscious of the emotional nature of the send off'. A couple of days later, they arrived in Rouen, via Southampton, their early romanticism shattered somewhat by an uncomfortable passage, during which they were 'packed like sardines'.

On arrival in France, Frank, Anthony and their friend Dick Breen were assigned to A Company and remained in that company for the duration of their time in France. Over the course of the next year, their experiences were dominated by the routines of war – digging trenches and making dugouts, doing ration runs and sentry duty. One of their early assignments, and one that was to recur throughout the first year, was to support those companies whose role it was to dig the underground tunnels, used to ferry explosives deep under the enemy lines. Known as 'sappers', many of these tunnelers had a background in mining. For Frank and his friends, however, this would have been a new experience. Their duties included hauling up the displaced chalk in sandbags and getting rid of the chalk in ways that would not alert the enemy; they also protected the saps by packing sandbags behind the explosives to prevent 'blowback' in the tunnel when the explosives were detonated. Working underground for eight hours a day, and 'white in body' from the chalky soil, they then had to march for at least an hour through mud-filled trenches to their dugouts. The winter of 1915 was notoriously bad and conditions in the trenches were horrific. Anthony describes the experience of living in 'four foot of slimy mud' and sleeping in 'rat-infested and lousy' dugouts which were rarely dry.

During that year, they also experienced time away from the trenches, when they were billeted in the small towns and villages of northern France, away from the front line, such as the village of Englebelmer, where they located for several months, returning to their 'comfortable quarters in a farm house' between 'jobs'. Most notably, in the spring of 1916, the platoon was given an extended break, travelling from town to town for about six weeks, a period that coincided with the 1916 Rebellion in Ireland, which, Brennan says, explains their long sojourn in the country for fear they would have a sympathetic reaction.

In the months leading up to the Battle of the Somme, the company moved closer to the front and the 'incessant rumbling of guns'. It became increasingly evident that preparations were being made for a major offensive. In the days before the battle commenced, as troops were massing behind the front lines, Brennan remembers the plentiful supply of rum and rations, and notes: 'We were being fattened for the slaughter. Some of us may have guessed it, but few could have thought that the Somme was to call for such a ghastly toll in human lives.'

Brennan's memoir describes the unfolding battle in graphic detail. The initial objective was to secure Mametz Wood. On that first day, 1st July 1916, they witnessed the movement of the 'Gordons' and the 'Devons' towards the front line, their pace so 'leisurely' that it was difficult to appreciate the reality of what was happening; this reality was made evident later when the Gordons began to collect their dead, forming a 'line of kilted corpses'. Days later, Brennan noted the high price paid for 'a few miles of ground', observing that there seemed to be 'a dead Devon in every shell-hole'. Later still, he was to comment on the fate of a newly arrived Welsh Division, who 'left their bones amongst the shattered trees' in Mametz Wood. Frank and Anthony, on the other hand, spent several days engaging in long treks with their company towards the woods to return to their billets, exhausted after a night spent involved in unsuccessful manoeuvres, diversionary tactics and 'confused and chaotic' attempts to traverse the dangerous terrain.

Billeted a few miles behind the line for almost a week, the platoon returned to the area around Mametz Wood to prepare for battle. Frank had just been promoted to Lance Corporal and Anthony was concerned that the friends would be separated, observing that: 'We had been inseparable since our arrival in France, and had shared many a hardship since then. We always bivouacked together; shared the same section of fours on route marches, and, in short, were really tried comrades.' The night before battle, the friends gathered on a hill near Mametz Wood and surveyed the shelling on the front line. They had been to Confession that afternoon and felt prepared for the next day. All were in good spirits, exchanging stories and banter until late into the night. Frank was, as Brennan describes it, 'as usual very eloquently laying down the law to a group of us'. Prompted by Mick Bergin, a friend from Callan, Co Kilkenny, the friends gradually moved backwards until Frank was standing alone at the centre of a 'ring of admiring listeners'. It took some time for him to realise that they were teasing him.

On the morning of 14th July, the friends stood waiting for battle at the edge of the wood, near the village of Bazentin-le-Petit. The battalion's scouts, led by Lieutenant Henry Harrison (a former MP (1890-92) and close ally of Charles Stewart Parnell), went ahead of them, including in their numbers their friend, George Buckley. Wishing him good luck, they watched as the scouts disappeared from view. George was killed minutes later. Frank and his comrades reached their target of Bazentin cemetery without encountering any opposition. Other companies of the battalion had taken possession of Bazentin-le-Petit. Convinced of their victory, the company let down their guard and walked outside the trenches, 'conversing and joking together'. Without warning, they came under machine-gun fire from an old windmill on a slope overlooking the cemetery. Everyone who could, dived for cover.

Brennan recalls that at that point, a small number of men, including Frank, under the leadership of Lt Dean, 'tried to rush the windmill'. Most were killed before the machine-gun was silenced. Eventually, the company was forced to withdraw temporarily from the cemetery. Anthony hadn't seen Frank since the battle had started and as soon as they had regained their position he began a frantic and fruitless search for him. Volunteering for a burial party, he continued to look for Frank without success, though he found several others, whose graves he dug in some distress. Soon after, planning to search the area around the windmill, he met the platoon stretcher-bearer, Tom Rowe, who told him that he had already looked among the dead at the windmill for Frank but that he wasn't there. Brennan didn't proceed further, something he subsequently regretted as, in hindsight, he believed Frank's body must have been there, probably made unrecognisable by post-mortem discolouration. Frank's body was never identified and he is among the names listed on the Memorial to the Missing of the Somme at Thiepval. His grief at Frank's death and at his inability to find his body is still palpable in the text written by Anthony Brennan over two decades later. He returned to the site of Frank's death in the 1930s on an unsuccessful mission to find the graves of dead friends. The windmill had disappeared at that stage and the pastoral scene he encountered was very distant from what he had experienced that day.

The memoir written by Anthony Brennan is imbued with the spirit of comradeship, stories of friends billeting together in the French countryside, experiencing the exhaustion of long marches and days spent underground, sharing jokes and rations in mud-filled dugouts and the nervous excitement of close calls in no-man's land. Frank's story is told in his best friend's voice, as close as we can get to understanding his life and death, a death that, according to family, his mother never accepted, viewing him as missing and likely to turn up eventually. There is some irony in the fact that we know more about Frank's experience of war than that of his older brother Bill, who survived the war. His obituary in the Longford Leader (22nd April 1950) described him as a 'most industrious worker and of a quiet disposition'. Wounded at the battle of Turee, he was 'mentioned in dispatches' and subsequently was awarded high military honour. There is some suggestion that after Frank's death, he was seen as culpable in setting the precedent for enlistment, though there is little evidence of this.

It is possible to find something of Frank's character in the memoir, particularly in the passage describing their last night together at Mametz Wood. Reading it for the first time was a profound experience; Frank was truly a Waldron, revelling in the power of words to captivate his audience, asserting his potential to lead – traits that emerged in the next generation, most notably in my father, Tom Waldron. On the day when we marked the centenary of Frank's death in Memorial Park, I read those words aloud and was ambushed once again by their emotional power and their capacity to conjure up Frank's presence, still nineteen and eager for the life ahead.

1 Myles Dungan, *They Shall Not Grow Old: Irish Soldiers and the Great War* (Four Courts Press, Dublin, 1997).
2 Imperial War Museum, London, Documents 12116, Anthony R Brennan, Private Papers.

Longmeadows • January

The Night Before

In memory of my grand-uncle,
Lance Corporal Francis (Frank) Waldron (1896-1916)

FIONNUALA WALDRON

You hauled the chalky earth
from tunnels, paths dug deep
beneath the hostile ground,
arteries into the enemy's heart,
emerging like a ghost
before your time, your skin
encrusted in the limey soil.

You marched in trenches filled
with grasping mud that sucked
your strength through rotting soles;
down lanes and roads
that smelled of living things,
through ruined towns laid bare
against the blood-red sky.

Each night you dreamt:
hot summers spent by water's edge,
your feet dipped in the cooling Nore.
Then, as daylight broke, you dreamt again:
lives suspended on the uncut wire,
the stink of fear, hovering
like bluebottles over bloated flesh.

The night before, you stood with friends
near Mametz Wood and built a fort of stories,
just like my father did a generation on,
– a legacy of sorts.
Next day, you took each step that led you
to that skirmish in the windmill,
where your story ended.

Pergola • July, January

Pergola • June, April

Fountain • December

Phoenix Park view • February

Viking Graves in the War Memorial Gardens

RUTH JOHNSON

I wrote this short synthesis on the Viking graves at the War Memorial Gardens during the Covid-19 pandemic in 2020, at which time the Gardens were a refuge for my family. Each day, around teatime, we walked to the riverside, approaching from one direction or another. Initially, the gate on Con Colbert Road was locked, and until the Office of Public Works reopened it, we would head through Liffey Gaels' pitch, with hurls and a ball, over the pedestrian bridge or via South Circular Road at Islandbridge. Another day we went up to the Phoenix Park and looked at the land from the other side, taking in the difference in levels, both in the valley and of the river itself on either side of the weir. The Inchicore and Kilmainham Viking burials had always interested me. I had assisted in some archaeological work near the War Memorial Gardens for the DART Underground railway project. When the National Museum was carrying out a rescue excavation where a Viking sword had been found, I had been down to look.

From the discovery of a small cemetery at the War Memorial Gardens in 1933-34 (the focus of this paper) to my appointment as City Archaeologist in 2001, no finds of Viking graves were reported in Dublin. From then on, the scene was to change as a result of increased urban renewal, archaeological development management, talented site archaeologists and a little luck. The first find, a disturbed warrior burial at Ship Street,[1] was made in testing at a small infill site in 2001. Other warrior burials were found at the edge of the Black Pool in advance of development on South Great George's Street in 2003. A high status woman of Scandinavian origin was discovered beside the church of St Canice in Finglas in 2004,[2] and a warrior was found at Golden Lane, beside the church and Christian cemetery of St Michael le Pole in 2007.[3] The chance discovery of a sword at Islandbridge was reported to the National Museum in 2004 and later excavated in 2008. This remarkable series of finds coincided nicely with the preparation by the National Museum of a detailed monograph on Viking graves from Ireland, of which there are 107 now recorded.[4]

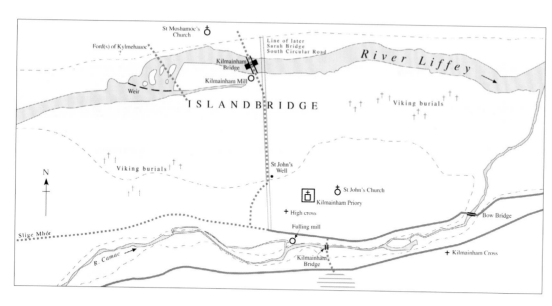

1 – Detail of map showing principal burial sites in medieval Kilmainham (from HB Clarke, Irish Historic Towns Atlas, 11 – Dublin, part 1, to 1610 (Royal Irish Academy, 2002)

opposite

2 – Watercolour by James Plunkett of Viking grave goods from Kilmainham, 1847

(© National Museum of Ireland)

These pagan burials speak of the Viking incursions of the 9th century. After a period of initial raiding at the end of the 8th century, a Viking naval force arrived on the Liffey in 837AD and the Norsemen became a permanent presence in Dublin from the winter of 841, when the Annals of Ulster tell us 'there was a naval camp at Duiblinn from which the Laigin [dynasties of Leinster] and the Uí Néill [dynasties of the midlands and the north] were plundered, both states and churches, as far as Sliab Bladma [Slieve Bloom mountains].'[5] Where exactly this camp (or longphort) was located is long debated by historians and archaeologists. So far the only archaeological evidence for 9th-century Viking habitation comes from the area near the Black Pool at the confluence of the Liffey and Poddle rivers around Dublin Castle and Temple Bar.

It has long been suggested, but not yet 'ground truthed', that an early Viking camp could have been located where the River Camac and the Liffey meet, between modern-day Heuston Station and Kilmainham/Islandbridge. There are parallels for the abandonment and relocation of Viking ship camps, for example at Woodstown in Waterford, which seems to have been relo-

cated upstream.[6] Kilmainham itself was an important place in early medieval Ireland before the Vikings arrived. It is named in the Triads, an early Irish text of the first millennium, as one of three places to land by ship. Irish sources record a major fording point at Kilmohauoc, overlooked from the northern bank of the Liffey by the Church of Mo Shamhóg and from the south by the church of St Maighneann, thought to have been located near Bully's Acre. Kilmainham's strategic importance is demonstrated by the fact the Battle of Dublin was fought there in 919 by Niall Glúndub (black knee) and the northern Uí Néill in an attempt to oust the Hiberno-Norse king, Sitric Caech, from Dublin. Its military significance was still evident in 1013 when Brian Boru and his army moved towards Dublin and set up a camp south of the River Liffey, from which they sacked and burned Clondalkin and Kilmainham and laid siege to Dublin. According to legend, Brian chose to camp at Kilmainham before the Battle of Clontarf in 1014.

In 1933 and 1934, while excavating in advance of the construction of the War Memorial Gardens, the workers found a small cemetery of five pagan graves oriented north-south where the western

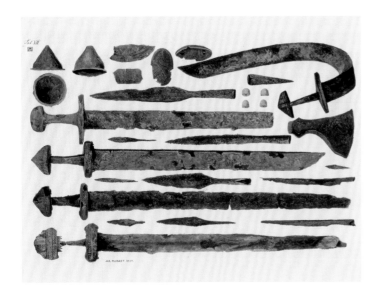

pond of the rose garden is now located. The associated weapons suggest that at least three of the burials were of warriors. This small cemetery was located on a north-facing slope overlooking the Liffey. A contemporary report in the *Irish Times* noted that a Christian cemetery, without any grave goods and with the skeletons laid east-west, of eight individuals had also been discovered close-by. This juxtaposition of pagan and Christian burial rite is not unique. Elsewhere in Dublin, Viking graves have been found close to contemporary churches and cemeteries, as at Finglas beside St Canice's church, and at Golden Lane and Ship Street, beside the church of St Michael le Pole.

The first find made during the construction of the War Memorial Gardens, in 1933, contained human remains, two swords, a spearhead, an axe-head, two iron 'staples', four nails and a 'slotted and pointed tool' of unknown use. The nails and staples are thought to have been part of a decayed wooden chest rather than a coffin. According to the *Irish Independent*, all the artefacts, except for one of the swords, came from a single grave.[7] It is possible that the more complete grave had been dug into earlier burial, which would explain the occurrence of the second sword.

Unfortunately, when the National Museum inspected the site the following day, the graves had been disturbed and the opportunity for scientific examination was lost. One of the swords found in 1933 was of an early type, measuring just under 1m, with a double-edged blade. Photographs of a second sword by the British Museum show an inscription on it, which is no longer visible.[8] The inscription reads ULFBERHT, a Frankish personal name used as a trademark by various blade-smiths operating in the Rhineland between the 9th and 11th centuries.

The second find, made at the Gardens in 1934, included the full skeleton of a man, equipped with a sword and spearhead. This time the excavation team comprised a captain from the Ordnance Survey, a military architect for the British Legion, and staff from the National Museum. Together with the workers, they bulk-lifted the burial in its soil matrix, placed it in a wooden box, and took it by horse-and-cart to the museum for controlled examination. Several black and white glass plate negatives record the excavations and operations in progress, and these are the earliest photographs of a Viking burial from Ireland.

The warrior found in 1934 has been on exhibition ever since, and is now in the Viking Gallery of the National Museum of Ireland on Kildare Street. Recent scientific analysis of the bones reveal that the individual had been a robust man in his twenties. He was approximately 6ft in height, which was tall by contemporary standards. He had an unusual and distinctive long and narrow skull, and had healthy teeth, though there is evidence that he suffered from bouts of malnutrition or parasites, leading to iron deficiencies. Furthermore, the vertebrae in his lower back show compression wear caused by physical activity, while the tops of his leg bones show signs of stress from horse-riding. In life he would have been an impressive and formidable sight, especially when fully equipped with weapons and mounted on horseback. In death, the hilt of the man's sword was placed on his upper chest with the point at his right knee, and the spearhead was placed at waist level on the left hand side of his body. The sword was broken into three pieces, perhaps in a deliberate ritual known as weapon mutilation, and may have been placed in a leather scabbard that did not survive. The double-edged sword measures approximately 93cm long, and has silver and bronze decoration on the guards. While the sword was an exotic import to Ireland, the spearhead is of a distinctly Dublin type.

The investigation in 1934 exposed the graves of another young person of unknown gender, an older man and a fourth individual of unknown gender, which had the jawbone of a cow placed beside their skull and their left arm raised in an unusual burial position. Animal bones are common occurrences in pagan Viking graves but the meaning behind their inclusion is obscure. In 1989, during the widening of Con Colbert Road, archaeologists found evidence for another pagan grave in the form of an Irish shrine hinge adapted for wear as a brooch. This brooch may have belonged to the War Memorial Garden cemetery but came from higher ground near the top of the steps into the War Memorial Gardens.

In the Viking Age, the small cemetery in the War Memorial Gardens may have been inter-visible with a burial found in 1843 in the Phoenix Park. This grave was on the north side of the Liffey on high ground somewhere between the Magazine Fort and the Wellington Memorial, overlooking the ford and close to the church and cemetery of Cill Mo Shamóg. The grave contained a woman with a pair of Scandinavian-type oval brooches of 9th-century date, and an Irish shrine mount of 8th-century manufacture adapted as a third brooch. Female burials of this type with sets of oval brooches and ornaments of modified Irish metalwork are known from western Norway, where they represent early contact between Scandinavia and the Irish Sea region. These women are considered by leading Norwegian scholars to be of high social status, in charge of managing the farms and households, while the men in their families were active overseas raiding and trading. The woman buried in the Phoenix Park was equally of high status and of Scandinavian descent, or identifying as Scandinavian culturally.

The War Memorial cemetery lies to the west of, and separate from, a much larger and very important burial ground focused around Islandbridge and Kilmainham. From 1785 onwards, finds from a large pagan cemetery had been reported by antiquarians at Kilmainham-Islandbridge, some half a kilometre to the east of the War Memorial Gardens. In 1860, a male grave containing weapons and a set of bronze scales was found by a local family quarrying for gravel in their backyard at Islandbridge. These artefacts were presented to the Royal Irish Academy, forerunner to the National Museum. Other finds of skeletons, along with items such as weapons, personal ornaments of Irish and Scandinavian types, fine weights and scales, horse equipment, tools and implements such as needle cases and purses were made in the area over a period of many years. This cemetery was spread over a large triangular area with burial clusters, perhaps reflecting different dates or discrete family groups. Analysing and mapping these old finds was a complex forensic exercise by numerous archaeologists, including Coffey and Armstrong in 1910, Boe in 1940, Hall and O'Brien in the 1990s, and, most recently, Harrison and O'Floinn.[9] The 53 burials at Kilmainham and Islandbridge make up approximately half of all known Viking graves from Ireland. The cemetery is the most important Viking burial landscape known outside Scandinavia and reflects the high number of Vikings operating raiding, slaving and trading in the Irish Sea.

The most recent discovery of a Viking burial in the vicinity of the War Memorial Gardens was from the grounds of the 1930s gate lodge at the Islandbridge entrance.[10] The burial had been disturbed in 2004, at which time a single-edged sword of early 9th-century Norwegian type and a spearhead of Dublin type were recovered. The excavation in 2008 revealed that this grave was of a young man, aged around 18 at the time of his death. Analysis of his teeth shows that he had moved to Ireland just prior to his death, probably from Scandinavia. He was wearing a copper-alloy ringed pin of Insular type, and was buried with a bronze scale-pan, of a type used for weighing silver in non-coin transactions. This burial was found on low ground, close to the river. As such it is considered to belong to the larger cemetery at Kilmainham and Islandbridge rather than the smaller cemetery in the War Memorial Gardens.

It is difficult to know what the pagan graves at the War Memorial Gardens, the Phoenix Park and at Islandbridge/Kilmainham looked like in the 9th century. Any surface features have been levelled over time. It is tempting to speculate that the graves would have had been covered by mounds of earth, as was the practice in Norway and elsewhere in Scandinavia. Such grave mounds would have been a prominent and distinctive feature marking the landscape as being under Viking control.

The number of pagan graves in the area around the War Memorial Gardens and the Kilmainham/Islandbridge area speak of a sub-stantial population of warrior elite operating out of Dublin Bay. Harrison and O'Floinn have observed the close correspondence between many Viking burial sites in Dublin and the boundaries of the later medieval liberty of Dublin. The 9th-century settlement at Temple Bar seems to have been ringed by Viking burials, many of which were located at critical access points such as roads and fords, and close to Christian churches. Why did the Vikings locate cemeteries at Kilmainham/Islandbridge, Inchicore and the Phoenix Park, two-and-a-half or three kilometres to the west of the Black Pool settlement? Perhaps the small cemetery in the Memorial Gardens was associated with a military outpost, a farm or was sited the edge of Viking territory in the 9th century. Only with strategic interdisciplinary research and focused archaeological excavations will we get closer to an answer.

_____

Endnotes

[1] Linzi Simpson, 'Viking warrior burials in Dublin: Is this the Longphort?', in Seán Duffy (ed.), *Medieval Dublin VI* (Four Courts Press, Dublin, 2005), pp.11-62. Linzi Simpson, 'The first phase of Viking activity in Ireland: archaeological evidence from Dublin', in John Sheehan and Donnchadh Ó Corráin (eds), *The Viking Age: Ireland and the west. Proceedings of the 15th Viking Congress, Cork, 2005* (Four Courts Press, Dublin, 2010). Linzi Simpson, 'Pre-Viking and early Viking-Age Dublin: research questions', in Seán Duffy (ed.), *Medieval Dublin X* (Four Courts Press, 2010).

[2] Maeve Sikora, 'The Finglas burial: archaeology and ethnicity in Viking-Age Dublin', in Sheehan and Ó Corráin (eds), *The Viking Age*. https://www.rte.ie/brainstorm/2020/1008/1170167-vikings-ireland-burials-dna-black-hair, accessed 14 May 2021.

[3] Ed O'Donovan, 'The Irish, the Vikings and the English: new archaeological evidence from excavations at Golden Lane, Dublin', in Seán Duffy (ed.), *Medieval Dublin VIII* (Four Courts Press, 2008), pp36-130.

[4] Stephen Harrison and Raghnall O'Floinn, *Viking Graves and Grave-Goods in Ireland* (National Museum of Ireland, 2014), pp.242-97.

[5] https://celt.ucc.ie//published/T100001A/index.html, acc. 14 May 2021.

[6] James Eogan (exec. ed.) et al, *Woodstown: A Viking-Age Settlement in Co. Waterford* (Four Courts Press, 2014).

[7] https://phoenixpark.ie/wp-content/uploads/2017/08/WM-CMP-PDF.compressed-1.pdf, accessed 18th May 2021. See also Harrison and O'Floinn, op. cit., pp.242-97.

[8] Haakon Shetelig (ed.), *Viking Antiquities in Great Britain and Ireland* (Oslo, 1940), p.62.

[9] George Coffey and ECR Armstrong, 'Scandinavian objects found at Islandbridge and Kilmainham', in *PRIAI, section C: Archaeology, Celtic Studies, History, Linguistics, Literature*, 28, 1910, pp.107-22. JSTOR, www.jstor.org/stable/ 25502780, acc. 19 May 2021. Johs. Boe, *Norse Antiquities in Ireland*, Part III *of* Haakon Shetelig (ed.), *Viking Antiquities*. Richard Hall, 'A Viking grave in the Phoenix Park, Co. Dublin,' in *JRSAI*, 104, 1974, pp.39-43. JSTOR, www.jstor.org/stable/25508641, acc. 19 May 2021. Elisabeth O'Brien, 'A reconsideration of the location and context of Viking burials at Kilmainham/ Islandbridge, Dublin', in Conleth Manning (ed.), *Dublin beyond the Pale: studies in honour of Paddy Healy* (Wordwell, Wicklow, 1998), pp.35-44. Harrison and O'Floinn, op. cit., pp.242-97.

[10] Maeve Sikora, Barra Ó Donnabháin and Niamh Daly, 'Preliminary report on a Viking warrior grave at War Memorial Park, Islandbridge', in Seán Duffy (ed.), *Medieval Dublin XI* (Four Courts Press, 2011).

Liffey heron • June

Longmeadows • March

Cedars • July

Linden blossom • July

Limes • April

Dreaming of Summer Blooms
at Longmeadows

A HAIBUN BY MAEVE O'SULLIVAN

After my working day, I escape from the laptop and its endless stream of emails, put my phone into airplane mode and fly through the football pitch opposite my home, across the pedestrian bridge over the dual carriageway and down the incline through the park's entrance. The sight of the Liffey lit by spring sunshine is an instant balm. Sometimes rowers slice their slim boats through the water, with guides cycling along-side, shouting instructions. At other times the winged ones have the river to themselves – ducks, swans and the occasional heron or cormorant.

> news bulletin
> I meet him in the park
> silent song thrush

I make my way down the path which runs alongside the river and up to the weir at Islandbridge, passing couples, families, and other solo walkers. From there, I look across to the big old house on the opposite bank, where I lived for seven years a couple of decades ago. I think about my life as it was then, and about my old housemates, all creatives. One of them, Jessica, an artist around my age, died of cancer last December. Two of her artworks hang in my apartment – a print depicting some fat fuchsias and a mirror that she made using pieces of my favourite mug which had fallen onto the tiled kitchen floor. Just before that we lost Blanaid, my late mother's best friend, and Olive, her favourite sister. A trio of fallen comrades. When I think about these three women, the first thing I remember is their laughter.

> winter fog
> over the river
> moving

It feels like this place is becoming a close friend. I need to check in with her every couple of days and see what's new. I observe her keenly, take comfort in her presence and try not to take her for granted. Some people refer to this time as a war, and, like the one on terror, the enemy — a tiny virus — is evasive. Paradoxically, these World War I memorial gardens have become a refuge from the ravages of this 2020 conflict, an antidote to the grim daily statistics and the feeling of being under siege. But the human history of this valley stretches back a millennium.

> Viking burial ground
> commemorating soldiers
> planted elsewhere

One of the lost soldiers was my great-uncle, Father Donal (DV) O'Sullivan. He answered a call from the Bishop of Kerry to serve as a chaplain to the forces in early 1916, and was killed by a shell on 5th July of the same year, in northern France, while giving last rites to another soldier who survived. He was 26. The diary found among his effects chart the few months he spent as a war chaplain. On 2nd July, he wrote: 'Masses along the front. German prisoners taken. Wounded, wounded, wounded! Ulster Division Rifles under heavy fire. Heavy casualties. Busy day for chaplains.' The memory of this young Killarney priest is lovingly cherished on my father's side of the family, and a number of us have visited his grave, located under a yew tree in a military cemetery just outside the small town of Bouzincourt.

> on his grave
> like in the old war song
> roses in bloom

Back in Islandbridge, Father Donal's name appears in the illustrated Roll of Honour, a log of the almost 50,000 Irishmen and women who lost their lives in the Great War. These manuscripts are kept in the book rooms placed at either end of two granite-paved pergolas, on which, towards the end of April, plentiful pink and white clematis stars give way to the pendulous wisteria blossoms, generously sharing their sweet scent.

Because of the unusually warm, dry spring, all the roses in the twin rose gardens are blooming early, peaking in June instead of July. The kaleidoscope of reds, pinks, oranges and yellows is drawing more visitors in now that travel restrictions have loosened. This early blossoming makes me feel slightly edgy: is it a sign that the summer is starting to gallop away too soon? I meet one of the gardeners one afternoon and compliment him on how good they're looking. 'That takes a fair bit of work', he says, nodding towards the display, 'lots of dead-heading.'

The four haiku in this haibun were first published in: Scott Mason (ed.), *Gratitude in a Time of Covid-19*, 2020 / *Haiku Spirit,* March 1999 / *Blithe Spirit*, Nov 2017 / *Blithe Spirit*, Aug 2010

Hawthorns • March

54

Hawthorns • May

Herbaceous border • January

Pergola • March

The importance of the
Irish National War Memorial

GALE SCANLAN

'6503 Private J Field, Royal Munster Fusiliers, 10th July 1918'. My family and I read these words on a tombstone within the beautifully kept Commonwealth War Graves cemetery at Südfriedhof, located about 5km south of the centre of Cologne in Germany. The tombstone is that of my husband Seán's grandfather. Seán and I, along with our daughters Saoirse and Bebhinn, travelled to Germany in late November 2015, partly as a pre-Christmas treat to soak up the atmosphere of the famous Christmas markets. However, we had deliberately chosen Cologne as our base in order to visit John Field's grave. This journey was long overdue, and Seán was the first member of his family to visit the grave of his maternal grandfather.

Seán's grandfather was born in Cork city on 19th November 1886. He married Mary Ellen Field at the Church of St Peter and Paul. Records show that they lived at 17 Harpur's Lane, Paul Street, in the 'Marsh' area of the city. He enlisted in the 2nd Bn Royal Munster Fusiliers in Tralee, probably in early January 1914, and along with many more immediately joined the battalion in Aldershot, Hampshire. The battalion sailed for France in August 1914 as part of the British Expeditionary Force (BEF) and experienced their first action at the Battle of Mons on 23rd August that year. The BEF was forced to retreat after some heavy German resistance known subsequently as the 'Retreat at Mons'. He and many of his fellow comrades were taken prisoner at Etreux on 27th August. They were sent first to Senne Prisoner of War (POW) Camp where conditions were appalling as the camp had not yet been completed. Records show that by 17th December he had been moved by rail to Limburg. Little is known after that, but further research indicates that by 17th May 1917 he was at Giessen POW Camp where he died. The only contact with his family during this time was through the heavily censored, and now faded, Red Cross postcards of the time.

John Field was shot dead during an escape attempt just eight weeks before the armistice. His widow remarried (his brother), and over time, as the political situation in Ireland grew more contentious, no one in the family spoke much of John, and his medals were safely tucked away and forgotten. As I stood watching my husband plant a small white bush by the grave in earth brought from Ireland, I thought of how this story would be familiar to so many families across Ireland and how John Field is numbered amongst those remembered at the Irish National War Memorial at Islandbridge. How different was this experience from that of my own grandfather, Private Thomas McCoy, Royal Inniskilling Fusiliers. With his friends who had joined up with him, he also fought in France but returned to a hero's welcome in his small village in Co Tyrone. In the coming years, he marched proudly wearing his medals in the annual commemoration ceremonies that followed.

Given these very personal connections, I felt honoured when invited to become a trustee of the Irish National War Memorial in 2007 by the then Chairman of the Trust, Maj Gen David The O'Morchoe CB CBE. As a retired British Army Officer originally from Northern Ireland, with a complex family background, I understand this to reflect in some small way the multiple identities of those whom the War Memorial Gardens commemorate. In 2013 I became honorary secretary and treasurer of the Trust on the death of our fellow trustee, Mr Frank Robinson (late Irish Guards), so I feel in a position to summarise the creation of the Memorial and to present its role in the 21st century.

Two weeks after the Treaty of Versailles was signed in July 1919, a hundred people attended a meeting at the Vice-Regal Lodge in the Phoenix Park (now Áras an Uachtaráin), where it was decided to establish a war memorial to commemorate the Irish war dead. A memorial committee was appointed and raised an initial £50,000 through public donations drawn from the whole of Ireland; it is amazing to consider that in today's money that would be equivalent to over €20.5m. While discussions about the location of a permanent war memorial were to take place over the following decade, our predecessors on the Trust set about an interim project to list the names of every Irish soldier who had lost

their life in the war. These Books of Remembrance were compiled, designed and produced during one of Ireland's most turbulent periods, against the backdrop of the War of Independence and the subsequent Civil War. They were finally published in 1923. Running to 3,200 pages and with almost 50,000 names and eight volumes, these records have the effect of humanising the war, something difficult to achieve due to the sheer scale of losses. As we are now approaching the end of the Decade of Centenaries Programme (2012-2023), which included anniversaries relating to WWI such as the Gallipoli landings, the Battles of the Somme and Messines, it is a measure of changing attitudes and times that several newly created Great War memorials have been built across the country in the last fifteen years in locations as diverse as Fermoy, Callan, Castlebar, Dungarvan and Glasnevin.

In 1929, the current location in Islandbridge was identified as a suitable location for the War Memorial. Trustee Andrew Jameson revealed to WT Cosgrave, President of the Executive Council, that he had already been in talks with Sir Edwin Lutyens, the foremost architect of the period, who had designed the Cenotaph in London, the Thiepval Memorial in France, and was architect to the Imperial War Graves Commission, with a view to commissioning a design. Impressed by Lutyens' designs and reputation, his proposal was recommended to Government and plans were finally approved in July 1931.

In late December 1931 work finally began, and even though the appetite for remembrances of the First World War in Ireland was declining, especially after the election of de Valera in 1932, work continued. A mix of ex-soldiers from both the British Forces and Óglaigh na hÉireann (Irish Defence Forces), many of whom had served in both armies, were employed to build the Memorial. This was visually important as the funds contributed by the Government to the scheme were drawn from the budget allocated to unemployment relief works. To ensure the maximum amount of labour available, the men worked with hand tools only, except for a steamroller and two concrete mixers. Having a professional interest in health and safety in the workplace, it was of particular interest to me to learn that despite using hand winches, steel ropes and pulley blocks to move the one-ton stones that make up the built features, only one workplace accident was recorded, and the person involved returned to work after three months. When you consider health and safety provisions of the time, that is quite an achievement.

From 1933, the Government did not take part in Armistice Day celebrations, and the sale of poppies, the wearing of British uniforms and flying of the national flag of the United Kingdom, the Union Jack, was restricted by law. The reality was that Armistice Day was being seen more and more as a British celebration, attracting the attention of radical nationalists, such as the destruction of the statue of George II in St Stephen's Green that same year. The War Memorial Gardens were finally completed in 1938, but the same concerns surrounded the issue of a formal opening of the Gardens, and although this was to take place in the summer of 1939, the thunder clouds of the Second World War were gathering, and it was postponed. Armistice Day celebrations did take place in the Gardens in 1940 and in the decades after that, but the planned formal opening never transpired.

The annual commemorations at the Gardens continued until 1971 when they were suspended and moved to St Patrick's Cathedral due to security concerns. Over the following years the site fell into disrepair as a lapse in the activity of the Memorial Committee, due to the death of some members, coincided with the economic downturn and cuts to the budget of the Office of Public Work (OPW), as well as the background of the Troubles in Northern Ireland. A new committee was formed in 1985 with members, as ever, drawn from north and south of the island, with the goal of addressing the condition of the Memorial.

This coincided with the economic and cultural shifts which were beginning to occur in Ireland during the mid-1980s and early signs of a change in the public's view of our national history and iden-

tity. Public opinion was shifting, as evidenced by the general outrage following the terrorist bombing during the Remembrance Sunday parade at the Enniskillen memorial in 1987. Restoration works were co-funded by the OPW and the National War Memorial Committee, and finally, on 10th November 1988, the restored Gardens were formally opened to the public after a delay of almost forty years. Since that date the Gardens have been consistently maintained, and an enormous debt of gratitude is owed to the OPW.

I want to conclude by referencing the Peace Process of the last twenty years and the impact this has had on the Memorial. The Peace Process in the 1990s transformed the relationship between the State and the memory of the war. For the first time, the Irish government was represented at the annual Remembrance Day service in St Patrick's Cathedral. Alongside these developments, the War Memorial was given a new profile and greater political importance. Three key pivotal moments stand out for me. Firstly, the unprecedented formal state commemoration of the 90th anniversary of the Battle of the Somme on 1st July 2006. This was attended by Uachtarán na hÉireann, Mary McAleese, Taoiseach Bertie Ahern, members of the Oireachtas, the diplomatic corps of the Allies of WWI, delegates from the Northern Ireland administration and political parties, and representatives of the four main churches, with a guard of honour drawn from Óglaigh na hÉireann. Secondly, during the first state visit by a British monarch to the Irish Republic on 18th May 2011, Queen Elizabeth II and President Mary McAleese, laid wreaths to commemorate Ireland's war dead of WWI and WWII. Finally, on 9th July 2016, the centenary of the Battle of the Somme, then Taoiseach Enda Kenny and President Michael D Higgins laid wreaths to honour Irish soldiers who fell in this battle.

The Islandbridge memorial has now gained official recognition at the highest level, providing a bridge between the past and present, a tangible expression of collective memory. It is not just a memorial to the war dead; it represents the physical site where the neglect of a particular tradition was played out. Through the commitment and expertise of the Office of Publc Works, the Memorial has become a designated Irish heritage site. It is a physical representation of our shared heritage. This shared heritage and the ongoing support and recognition of it takes on additional contemporary relevance and importance against the backdrop of Brexit and the concerns and challenges it presents to both north-south and east-west relations. Representation on the Trust of the Irish National War Memorial is drawn from the whole of the island of Ireland. This is embedded in the Trust Deed, and it is critical to the success of the ongoing work of the Trust and our ability to remain relevant in providing a conduit and opportunity for dialogue and agreed actions to protect and raise awareness of the Memorial, our shared heritage and common history.

During the reciprocal state visit to the United Kingdom in 2014, President Higgins referenced Thomas Kettle, the Irish nationalist and poet who is one of the best-known victims of the Battle of the Somme. President Higgins' words had powerful contemporary resonance, capturing the complexities of the Memorial and those it commemorates when he described Thomas Kettle as 'an Irish Patriot, a British soldier and a true European'. These words are a testimony to the time and are as valid and true today.

To my Daughter Betty, the Gift of God

In wiser days, my darling rosebud, blown
To beauty proud as was your mother's prime,
In that desired, delayed, incredible time
You'll ask why I abandoned you, my own,
And the dear heart that was your baby throne
To dice with death. And oh! they'll give you rhyme
And reason: some will call the thing sublime,
And some decry it in a knowing tone.
So here, while the mad guns curse overhead,
And tired men sigh with mud for couch and floor,
Know that we fools, now with the foolish dead,
Died not for flag, nor King, nor Emperor,
But for a dream, born in a herdsman's shed,
And for the secret Scripture of the poor.

Thomas Michael Kettle (1880-1916)
dated 'In the field, before Guillemont, Somme, Sept. 4, 1916'

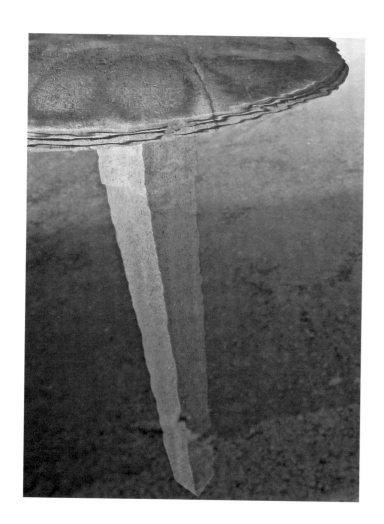

Reflections • June, August

Reflections • September, August

Fountain • May, March

Riffles • September

Sunset • July

Safe Shall Be My Going

ANNE TANNAM

There's the shadow of young Ned
from his vantage point on the top step,
watching the other children hurl their bodies
off the edge of a granite wall, offer themselves
to gravity's mercy, landing in laughing, tangled
piles of limbs, before racing up the steps
to begin the game again.

> There's the river, nodding at Ned, reminding him
> that long, long before the Imperial British Empire,
> Viking children played along her sandy banks,
> their voices carrying upwind, whispering to the earth
> Nordic tales of war and ice, while fathers washed
> blood from swords, laid out the fallen bodies for burial.

There's Ned, before he is Edwin, before his eyes map
these gardens; position the pavilions, the pergolas,
the book rooms, the temple, the fountains;
before Flanders fields where *poppies blow*
between the crosses row on row; before Harry,
in black ink, sketches seven silhouettes, each one
a shadow grave in which to lay the limp and broken bodies
of the Irishmen *who went as they were asked.*

> There's the shadow of Edwin,
> sitting silent at the base of the war stone,
> seeking *safety with all things undying,*
> watching the sky soften into darkness,
> as he waits for morning, when the children
> will come, strong-limbed and racing
> across the long meadow, laying their claim
> to this day's *freedom and the autumnal earth.*

Sunken garden • July

Sunken garden • January

South-east portico • July

Boy Soldiers

AT THE IRISH NATIONAL WAR
MEMORIAL GARDENS

ANNEMARIE NÍ CHURREÁIN

i   Let us remember John—son of Catherine,
who at fourteen years old weighed eight stone and a half

—the boy from Wheelbarrow Lane,
the boy who ran the streets of Waterford putting it all up to the Gods,
a hurley stick against the sun.

He was killed in World War I
by the burn of enemy gas rising cloud-like into his eyes,
        through his father's eyes,
              and his father's father's eyes.

In our deepest gardens, we have built an amphitheatre
with our grief. We have wounded ourselves
into the earth and each year, we kneel
to inhale the roses.

In his honour, the stone inscription reads
with all things undying, we have found safety.

ii   Let us forget the unnamed son
of the unnamed mother who was found slumped over a leaf of foil.
        One touch and he knew—she was *gone.*

He was raised by his uncles to become
a look-out boy. On the outer edge of Dublin city,
        where once the Cambro-Norman knights rode on horses,
he rode his bicycle in the rain.

At the age of eighteen, he was led through the fourth province
of the rosarium
and among the petals, he was shot
        three times in the skull.

They turned the lining of his pockets inside out
and left him for dead.

In court it was said: *he was a cog in the wheel.*
The newspapers ran the headline: *he had been warned.*

West pond • September

The World is Calling

JEAN O'BRIEN

A morning walk in what was once the Long Meadow
takes me along the wide expanse of the Liffey
as it advances past Islandbridge and on into the city
and then the sea. I turn from my city's Plurabelle river
up to Lutyens' Memorial gardens
to see the formal rose garden with its riot of colour,
the reds and yellows atop thorny stems, brute beauty
and valour as Hopkins had it.

The granite Book Rooms reflecting the sun's indifference,
four huge, impenetrable sarcophagi holding the books
that list the slaughtered, ordered architectural features
masking and making polite the sending of young men
out to die. Nothing here in this memorial speaks
of the horrors endured before they died,
and always women left behind, bereft of sons,
brothers and husbands; they never wanted this.

The only colour now amid all the granite grey,
apart from blazoned roses in the sunken garden below
are the barrage of blood red poppy wreaths,
like the flow of blood, bones and marrow that fertilised
the fields of Flanders and Pilckem Ridge in Passchendaele
where our poet Ledwidge of the blackbirds and the bitterns fell.

> *The lost ones scattered wide,*
> *Give me your hand. O brother, let us go*
> *Crying about the dark for those who died.*

> – from 'The Lost Ones' by Francis Ledwidge

Willow • July, March

War Stone • June

Dead Soldiers Remembered: Uncertainty

SHEILA GORMAN

In both the Great War and World War II, each soldier was accompanied by uncertainty. They did not know if they would see their families again, if they would embrace their wives or children in the future. The unmarried wrote to their families, especially to their mothers. In the Great War some soldiers were given postcards to fill in which would give no information about where they were or which regiment they were with. On these postcards they were instructed to cross out what did not apply. 'I am in hospital. I have been wounded. I am in good health.' But they were all the while uncertain.

In the Great War, when they waited in the trenches for the whistles to blow, they did know they would be shot dead by their own officers if they did not go over the top. They must obey orders. When they climbed out of their trenches they did not know if they would return unhurt, be injured or killed by the enemy. Each day might be their last day.

Each day as the war progressed, the men feared and doubted. They feared annihilation. They feared letting down their colleagues and their regiment. They feared not being able to be courageous. Despite their training they doubted their own behaviour. Could they be heroes? Would they be brave? They also feared the enemy.

Being part of a smaller group, a regiment or patrol, was important. It helped men to feel they belonged. This could be balanced against their doubt of not behaving as was expected of them. Each man was dressed the same as his colleagues. They wore the uniform of the British Army. Their uniforms bound them together as a fighting force. The uniform helped them to feel they belonged. They were trained to know their role. But still they were uncertain.

But sometimes aspects of their uniforms also made them targets. The enemy snipers were taught to aim at the men 'with the thin knees'. The officers wore jodhpurs. These flared out at the hips and in at the knees. To kill an officer was more effective than killing an ordinary soldier. After all, officers gave the orders. The other ranks obeyed them. In the late stages of the Great War, officers swopped their jodhpurs for the trousers and puttees of their men. This made them safer, but not impervious to injury or death.

Many of the men were young. Some had lied about their age to enlist. Still children. Thought that they were going to have an adventure, play a bit. But the shells were not playing. They were real, not toys, and exploded amongst the men. Killing and maiming. Their uniforms did not save them. They were not issued with steel hats until 1917.

The noise was terrific. The incoming shells whistling, crashing to earth and exploding, the crack of bullets from the enemy's rifle fire. Never knowing if they were the one that would be hit. Injured or maybe killed. They learned to live with the constant uncertainty. They learned not to think about the future. They knew they may not have one.

Some other sounds were the rattling, overbearing, overhead barrages of their own guns. This was fired before going over the top of the trench. It was aimed at the enemy barbed wire in front of them, trying to destroy it. It rarely did. This barbed wire resulted in many deaths.

Later it was learned by the leaders that the uniforms of the dead sometimes helped the enemy. Then the leaders ensured that before a big push, the men would remove any items like cap badges or insignia or other emblems of allegiance which might give information to the enemy. They did not want the enemy to see these clues on the dead after the battle. They did not want the enemy to know which regiment was fighting where. Sometimes these emblems were replaced by battle patches sewn to the back of the uniform. This meant that the men could be identified by their own regiment but not by the enemy.

The uniforms of both sides – the khaki of the British and the grey of the German – made each side see the other as less than human. The Germans were called 'rats' by the British. This meant that each side had the ability to treat the other with less moral responsibility. This made shooting and killing easier.

The smell was of the blood and the dead. Men and horses. The men could almost taste the metal of shell casings and the decay. Earth and uprooted and blasted trees. Smell and taste became confused. Many of the dead were caught on barbed wire which had not been cut as promised by their officers. The wire had been unrolled by the enemy to prevent anyone crossing no-man's land to reach them.

Some of the men had been used to working outdoors. Those who worked on farms and with animals, for instance, were used to being outside in all weathers, in the dark of the early mornings and evenings and the light of the day. Others had been in offices and so unused to outdoor life. Unused to the colour of earth. The sound of the wind in the trees. Those used to the outdoors found it a little easier.

Every dead soldier, whatever his origin, was remembered by his family, by his regiment and by his army.

_____

Book rooms • June

Memorial lawn • November

Memorial lawn • February

Magnolia • April

A Garden for my Grandfather

RITA DUFFY

The Memorial Gardens will always be a special place in Dublin for me. I spent time there thinking about my life – facing myself during a world pandemic and grappling with the challenges that transform a life. Covid 19 blasted in from nowhere, gathering pace as it whipped around the globe and smashed all our doors closed in its deadly draught. Fear circled, we went into lockdown and were warned to stay apart. We washed our groceries, sanitised the door bell and listened to stories about the Spanish flu. In the evenings we crocheted little squares, death tolls mounted, as each beautiful little woollen piece was snipped free of its moorings and added to the pile, like expendable men in uniform walking towards enemy trenches.

It was spring, and like every other living thing I felt the urge to move and reach out beyond myself. I decided to start jogging. I'm not a natural runner. I smeared on lipstick, smiled at myself in the mirror and off out I went. Each day, I arrived at the Memorial Park, stopping and starting, down under the trees, then veering to the right on a carpet of lush spring grass. Van Morrison playing in my ears 'in the garden, all misty wet with rain'. I wiped the sweat from my brow and passed under the long pergola with its canopy of almost-ready-to-bloom clematis.

I had been in the Memorial Park before and admired the ordered beauty of Lutyens' design; this time I claimed it as my own. Each day I appreciated its open availability, and each day that circular garden ringed me round in an energetic embrace. Uplifting spring sunshine cut shadows on perfect stone work. I breathed deeply and pooled my thoughts. Each panting orbit of the circular path was a triumph, marked by the laying down of a small twig. I focused on the ball of granite held aloft amid the magnolia blossom, a version of our troubled planet, crowning the wall. I paced myself and tried to forget my feet and my struggle.

I began to think about my grandfather Duffy who died at the Somme in 1916. He was a man I never knew. I keep his photo on my computer and I know the family story. In this garden, I begin to imagine I am running on the edge of his pocket watch. I portion the ground to make each rhythmic circuit more manageable. I stop for breath and walk from 'half past' to a 'quarter to', the hands of the clock radiating from the little sunken pond at the centre of the garden. A garden of perfect circles pressed accurately into the ground like a reversed wedding cake, layers fortified by stone and punctuated by small nestling benches. I remembered an image of a small lake I'd seen while travelling former battle fields in Belgium. I was told of a bomb blast so huge it scooped out the earth and the crater filled with water. The seismic tremor was supposedly felt in southern England, like the exaggerated deed of some Cúchulainn, a battle-warp shifting of landscape and limb.

In 2016 I was commissioned to present *The Souvenir Shop* project, a contemporary art installation close to the site of Proclamation signatory Thomas Clarke's tobacconist on Parnell Street, beside Belvedere College in Dublin. I included in this project my grandfather's Somme medal and my grandmother's letter. This page sent from the front, written by HV Gill sj, a Jesuit priest who was an army chaplain, having formerly taught at Belvedere. How many times have I read that letter? Exploring the century-old words, skeletal arms of reversed type, hammered onto paper. The red and blue ribbon, a backdrop of battle

2/ R. Irish Rifles,

British Expeditionary Force,

France.

5/9/16.

Dear Mrs Duffy,

        I hope you will pardon me for not writing to you sooner, to tell you how sorry I was and am about your great loss in losing your husband. He was a brave and good man.

    Whenever there was difficult or dangerous work to be done he was always in it, and more than once his Company Commander singled him out for praise.

    He came regularly to the Sacraments and to our Evening Devotions, He was one of those I knew best and I was grieved indeed to hear of his death.

    God will comfort you and help you to bear the great loss. He has his own good object in all the suffering it allows.

    Your Husband lived a good life and died a Hero's death, that will not make your sorrow less, but it will help you to bear it in resignation to God's will, Who, does not even allow a sparrow to fall without his Providence.

    As you perhaps know your husband was a bomber, and had difficult and important duties. He was shot when taking part in the attacks made by this battalion in the beginning of July. He only lived a few minutes after he was shot and can have suffered but little pain, He always went to Confession and Holy Communion before an attack, now you may therefore be at ease about him. God will comfort you and one day you will meet him again in our Eternal Home, with deepest sympathy,

                I remain,

          Yours very sincerely,

             H.V.Gill. S.J.

landscape, pulled across the page, occasionally leaving licks of red under the letters g and y. One day during the Souvenir Shop project, the archivist from Belvedere visited. Amongst the artifacts and collections, he found the letter; his enthusiasm lit up the room: I had a fragile link, a thread spooling down through the years. HV Gill was a scientist, interested in measuring the impact of explosions, the archivist told me. He had once given a lecture at Cambridge and was really more interested in science than teaching; he had used a spinning top to illustrate his lecture. I felt that rare feeling artists recognise, a synergy that opens linear time, permitting two dead men to walk through a century and appear before me.

Researching for the Souvenir Shop project, I had purchased a tin toy, curious about its potential. I played with it occasionally. In the end it remained motionless on my studio desk: a spinning top. HV Gill mentions in the letter he knew my grandfather, was obviously a man with a solid belief in his God, and I imagine him, a compassionate man, writing that letter for my grandmother in a dugout shelter amidst bombs and gunfire. An all-attentive God 'who would not let a sparrow fall from a branch without his knowing', and the letter reads like he really did know and care about her husband, my grandfather.

The Memorial Park is an elaborate war memorial, perfect in proportion and intended to commemorate our fallen dead. Irishmen who fought for the freedom of small nations, many of them too poor to be patriots. Running in the heart of this glorious garden I considered my own family story. My father was six when he ran, with his siblings and mother, away from the burning wreckage of their Belfast home. His father was four years dead and gone and ploughed into the Somme's cloying muck. No quarter was given to his family, in a city thrown off kilter by revolutionary desire for the freedom of this small nation. They were Catholics and judged 'other' by a band of men with a barrel of beer. They were not permitted by their neighbours to live on the Shankill end of Conway Street, but, fortunate enough to know the bonds of fam-

ily a few streets away, they found refuge with my great aunt Mary in Albert Street. Secure, behind St Peter's Cathedral, 'stay amongst your own' was the phrase they learned.

A few years later, my grandmother Margaret loaned her ardently Republican brother-in-law enough money from her war widow's pension to open a builders' yard. This happened shortly after his release from internment on the prison ship *SS Argenta*, moored in Belfast Lough. He was one of 700 other Catholic men under suspicion and rounded up and put into cages below deck. Partition had divided the island, and Belfast was at bitter odds with itself. A vicious drama played out in the North, and, as we know today, it never quite ended. My great-uncle made a success of the opportunity inadvertently delivered by king and country, and along with other newly isolated nationalists, he navigated sectarian waters, swimming to the shore of financial stability in a tremulous city thrown off kilter by partition.

An enduring result of my uncle's success was the education of his son Francis, a clever boy who thrived in the pigeon loft his father transformed into a study. He went to Queen's University to study literature. He chose his own course of study, in ancient Irish literature. Like the scholars of old, he taught himself all the Celtic languages, researched early manuscripts and began the Irish Studies Department at Queen's University, Belfast. He took back his own name, Proinsias Mac Cana, and moved on with brilliance in a rapidly changing world.

I love the circularity of this family story. There is real human courage. Women loyal to family rather than empire are cast as heroes; education, not violence, sets us all free.

————

opposite – Letter to my grandmother from army chaplin, HV Gill SJ, 5 Sept 1916

West pond • January

West pond • August

West pond • November

East pond • January

Sunset • July

A Place of Ritual and Memories

NUALA HAYES

snapshot **1** The Quickening

July 1976. There is a heatwave in Ireland and I am nine months pregnant. On the tree-lined avenue parallel to the River Liffey, our almost three-year-old son, Oisín, cycles his tricycle with my husband, Art Ó Briain, by his side, and I feel the first signs that the new baby is about to be born. I can still point out the bush where the journey began. We are considering a move to this side of the city. We had to make a quick decision given the circumstances. We decided to go for it, just as Eoin was about to arrive in the world. I did not know then that almost a lifetime later I would still live close by the river, or that the Memorial Gardens at Islandbridge would become my personal oasis for reflection and relief from the stresses of life in the city.

snapshot **2** Dereliction

Walking from our house in Railway Cottages, Inchicore, or the Works, as the CIÉ estate was known, through the park on the way to the river. Wild horses graze on the green lawns. The bushes, the sunken rose gardens and shrubberies are overgrown and neglected. The cross of the Altar of Remembrance has been broken. The fountains are filthy and dry. Old beer cans, newspapers, graffiti and evidence of late-night drinking parties are scattered and blown beneath the columns and crevices. The air is thick with fog and the smell of coal smoke from thousands of Dublin chimneys. The gated park has become a sad, gloomy place where beauty has faded through neglect and lack of appreciation.

Having grown up on the south side of the city, I knew nothing of the history of the Memorial Park and of its importance in the story of Dublin, of the Viking burial ground, or of Lutyens, the famed architect of the British Empire.

To local people, our neighbours in the Railway Houses, who were mainly the families of employees in the CIÉ works, the park was known as the Legion Park.

The British Legion were believed at the time to be the custodians of the Memorial Park. The original skilled workers of the Great Southern and Western Railway Works came from England and were provided with houses, a school and churches of different denominations, still evident along Inchicore Road. Many of these original families would have identified with, and some were involved in, the horrors of World War I, which resulted in the loss of so many young lives.

The pieties of the Catholic republic in which we grew up in Ireland from 1937 did not include ritual memories of the British occupation, and so the park as a symbol was neglected and overlooked by the new state.

snapshot 3 *Ceol, Dúchas agus Dóchas*: Music, Heritage and Hope

It's the 1980s, and although work and money is scarce there has been a revival of interest in traditional music and song. The voices of singers such as Christy Moore, Mary Black and Paul Brady, and the music of Donal Lunny and Moving Hearts soar over the park to lift the spirits of all who sit on the grass to listen with their children, dogs and families.

Féile Inse Chór (Inchicore Festival) has been set up to reflect the cultural awakening of interest in the Irish language in Dublin 8. Gael Scoil Inse Chór was founded by local people, including our family, to provide education through the medium of the Irish language for the children of Inchicore and Ballyfermot. The only space in the area suitable for building such a school was right beside the Memorial Park, near where there were football fields and a sports club. However, the Office of Public Works would not agree at that time to release the land.

At this point, the Office of Public Works had begun the restoration of the park. The monument has been restored, as have the

two circular sunken rose gardens designed by the landscape gardener Gertrude Jekyll, with pergola and lily ponds to the east and west of the ritual monuments. The fine dry stone walls created by some of the best stonemasons in Ireland at the time are now visible again. The annual Remembrance Day Commemoration takes place each year in November, and slowly the people of the area are becoming aware of the significance of this beautiful place, conceived as an extension of the Phoenix Park which hugs the ever moving river – Anna Livia Plurabelle, as Joyce remembered her.

snapshot 4 *Fianaise*: Bearing Witness – The Millennium

It's the year 2000 AD. The turning from 20th to 21st century is a time for reflection. The future is unknown. We look back for revelation, and the light shone on the painful shadows of our past reveals much of what has been hidden. Known but not spoken about. I was involved, along with others, in an oral history project called *Fianaise*, set up by a local development group and supported by Dublin City Council.

It was my privilege to spend time with and record the memories of local people who had lived through the century and who were willing to share their memories for future generations. If there was a thread connecting these stories, it was of a community who survived extreme poverty, two world wars and the struggle for independence from Great Britain with resilience, community values and family solidarity. 'Nobody had anything, but what they had they shared', as Bob Fitzpatrick, born in 1917 and who grew up on Tram Terrace in Goldenbridge, remembered. He was 83 when I met him, and for over three hours he shared his detailed memories. He vaguely remembered the old soldiers, dressed like Chelsea Pensioners, who lived in the Royal Hospital and who would sit on a log outside a pub on the third lock of the canal on a fine day.

He remembered 'Gosh' Ryan, an ex-British soldier who wandered the streets, shell-shocked. Each year 'Gosh' had to go to Beaumont Hospital to be 'certified' in order to keep his British Army pension. According to Bob, some local young men had joined the British Army in order to survive and support their families, and the war took its toll on many of them.

Young women often chose a marriage of convenience to a soldier, which was looked upon locally, according to Bob, as a 'nine-day wonder'. The security of the pension was as big an attraction as anything else. When I asked Bob about the attitude of local people to the British Army, he thought for a while and then answered cautiously, 'fifty-fifty'.

snapshot 5 2011: A Visit from the Queen of England

A knock on the door. Two men stand there. One in front smiling, the other two steps behind unsmiling. Watchful. They introduce themselves as representing An Gárda Síochána. I had guessed as much: Good Cop / Bad Cop.

— How many windows had I in my house?
— Well, I answered, three in the front and four in the back. Why?
— Was I aware of the upcoming visit of her Majesty Queen Elizabeth to Ireland?
— Indeed, I am, I replied.
— And what are your views on her visit? The question came from the non-smiling Garda.
— I have no views whatsoever on that matter, I reply, but I'm sure she will be made feel very welcome.

The smiling Garda then passes me the timetable of the dates when vehicular access to our houses will be restricted as Her Majesty will visit the Memorial Gardens and Áras an Uachtaráin in the Phoenix Park – with apologies in advance for any inconvenience.

The visit of Queen Elizabeth for four days in 2011 is now history. It was a great success, part of the process to create peace, and

marking a new and cordial phase in the complex relationship between our two islands.

I watched the ritual on television. Her Majesty joined President Mary McAleese at the Garden of Remembrance in Parnell Square and laid a wreath below the huge sculpture of the Children of Lir, in memory of those who lost their lives in the fight for Irish independence. Then both women, representing our two nations, reciprocated the gesture at the Memorial Gardens by placing a wreath at the foot of the altar in memory of 49,400 Irishmen who lost their lives during the Great War. It seemed at last that 'Hope and History would rhyme', a phrase coined by Seamus Heaney.

Notable at the ceremony was the presence of unionists from Northern Ireland and republicans from Sinn Féin. The Peace Process that brought an end to thirty years of war in the North, had resulted eventually in the laying down of paramilitary arms from both sides. The occasion was even more notable for the inclusion of Northern Protestant paramilitaries, representatives of the UDA and UVF, organisations which had been the source of great fear and deep resentment from a large section of the community. They also were part of the symbolic ending of a very painful part of our shared history. Wreaths of red poppies at the Memorial are now accepted by all who use the park for recreation and remembrance.

snapshot 6 November 2019

Leaves slowly drift from the trees. Dogs and their owners socialise in designated areas.

Children from Gael Scoil Inse Chór, now a well-established school in the area, play hurling and camogie in the field beside the park. Groups from St John of God's School take the fresh air along by the river. The resident swans and ducks benefit from the growth in population all around the park. Apartment blocks have replaced the old mills and army barracks in Islandbridge. A new multicultural generation lives in the area, visits the park, enjoys its beauty unencumbered by the old myths, beliefs and traditions.

They may not know the story of the origin of the pair of swans on the river, that the swans were a gift from WB Yeats and Oliver St John Gogarty to the river in gratitude for saving the life of Gogarty when he was about to be assassinated by republicans during the Civil War in 1923. He was kidnapped and held in a house beside the Liffey, opposite the site of the Memorial Gardens. He escaped from his captors by jumping into the river and swimming to freedom. An offering of swans to the river was a symbolic gesture at the end of that terrible Civil War. In his poem 'To the Liffey with the Swans', Gogarty wrote:

> Keep you these calm and lovely things,
> And float them on your clearest water;
> For one would not disgrace a King's
> Transformed, beloved and buoyant daughter.
>
> And with her goes this sprightly swan,
> A bird of more than royal feather,
> With alban beauty clothed upon:
> O keep them safe and well together !
>
> As fair as was that doubled Bird,
> By love of Leda so besotten,
> That she was all with wonder stirred,
> And the Twin Sportsmen were begotten !

It's November, Samhain in the ancient Celtic calendar. Now is the time of remembrance for the living and the ghosts of the past hover but don't linger, unless we invite them to stay.

———

St John Gogarty poem reprinted by kind permission of the Gogarty estate

Pergola • March

North terrace • April

North terrace • November

Reflection • April

Heron • October

War stone • July

Reflecting on the Architectural Context of the INWMG

ANGELA ROLFE

During my daily walks through the Irish National War Memorial Gardens (INWMG), over the past twelve months, my appreciation of this extraordinary collaborative project has grown. The Gardens represent a remarkable shared vision, not only to build a memorial to those who died, but to create a significant place to give solace and an enduring legacy for subsequent generations. The quality of the architecture and extraordinary sense of place has proved resilient during times of neglect and indifference, and is now embedded with new layers of meaning and humanism.

For more than forty years I had accepted the narrative that the Memorial Gardens were deliberately hidden away, disconnected from the city centre and a local community – an embarrassing reminder of a bygone time. FX Martin in his essay '1916 – Myth, Fact and Mystery' refers to a national amnesia and writes, 'in independent Ireland it was difficult to find men and women who will acknowledge that they are children of the men who were serving during 1916 in the British Army'.[1] So it seemed inevitable that the Memorial Gardens would be neglected and vandalised during the decades of the Troubles. Between 1977 and 1988 I viewed the Gardens as a picturesque, almost romantic ruin or a folly in an alien place. As a recently qualified architect, I had visited an important retrospective exhibition, *Lutyens: the Work of the English Architect Sir Edwin Lutyens (1869-1944)*, at the Hayward Gallery, London, in 1981-82 that was to make him an icon of the post-modern movement. However, in 1981, the hunger strike by republican prisoners in Northern Ireland generated anti-British sentiments: it was not a time to discuss this place.

My appreciation of Edwin Lutyens started much earlier, because, like Lutyens, I spent my formative years in a village in West Surrey, where, more than a hundred years earlier, he was free to roam the countryside, sketching vernacular buildings and craftsmen at work, which would inform his architectural approach and philosophy throughout his long career. Edwin Lutyens was born in 1869. Hs father was a retired captain in

1   Published in *Studia Hibernica*, no. 7, 1967, pp.7-126.

the British army and a professional painter, and his mother, Mary Theresa Gallwey, was originally from Killarney. Edwin was the tenth child and ninth boy of their thirteen children. Edwin, always known as Ned, was a delicate child due to a bout of rheumatic fever. As a result, he did not attend public school or university; he shared his sister's governess and received extra schooling from his brothers. In 1885 he enrolled at Kensington School of Art, but left after two years to become a paying apprentice in the offices of Ernest George and Harold Peto, the designer of the Italian Gardens on Garinish Island, Co Cork.

At the age of 20, Edwin Lutyens set up his own architectural practice in London. His clients were wealthy businessmen looking for small country homes in West Surrey. Through them, he met garden designer, Gertrude Jekyll (1843-1932), 25 years his senior, who was to have a pivotal influence on his architectural career. Jekyll's training, also at Kensington Art School, had been in embroidery and silverwork; she was inspired by William Morris who had pioneered the English Arts and Crafts Movement and famously said, 'Have nothing in your house you do not know to be useful or believe to be beautiful.' When Jekyll's eyesight began to fail she took up garden design, influenced by William Robinson, an Irish gardener and journalist who popularised the English cottage garden. She began to create her own garden at Munstead Wood and asked Lutyens to design her a house within it. He created a house exemplifying the principles of the Arts and Crafts Movement, using traditional crafts, local knowledge and materials in perfect harmony with the setting.

In 1897 Lutyens married Lady Emily Lytton and together they moved to Bloomsbury Square, London, from where he ran his practice. Emily introduced a number of influential clients, including Edward Hudson, founder of *Country Life* magazine, bringing many more house and garden commissions. The Lutyens-Jekyll partnership was a synthesis between architecture and garden design, an integration of building and landscape, a dynamic composition of constructed gardens linked by precisely defined vistas, combining pavilions, pergolas and water features with terraces, stairways and sunken gardens, complementing Jekyll's planting perfectly. In 1906 they designed a garden for Heywood House, Co Laois, consisting of many of these elements, in classical form, that would later shape the design of many cemeteries and memorials on the Western Front, and ultimately the INWMG in Dublin.

During the Great War, Edwin Lutyens, together with two well-established Victorian architects, Herbert Baker and Reginald Bloomfield, was appointed architect to the Imperial War Graves Commission.[2] Between 1917 and 1930, Lutyens designed and supervised 140 cemeteries in Flanders, 49 memorials in Britain and nine around the world, including Ireland. In a report to the War Graves Commission, Lutyens stated that while it is 'important to secure the qualities of repose and dignity, there is no need for cemeteries to be gloomy or sad-looking places.'[3] He sought advice from Jekyll on 'the best and most beautiful flowering plants'.[4] Lutyens' best known memorials are the Cenotaph in Whitehall, London, and the Memorial to the Missing at Thiepval in France.

In 1919 a memorial committee was appointed in Ireland to raise funds for a suitable memorial. First they commissioned Ireland's Memorial Records, which lists the name of every known Irish soldier who had been lost in the war. The eight volumes, which include just under 50,000 names, were completed between 1919 and 1923. The very best of Irish artisans were involved in the production, and Harry Clarke, already highly regarded for his work in book illustration and stained glass, was commissioned for the

2 Imperial War Graves Commission changed its name to the Commonwealth War Graves Commission in 1960 (www.cwgc.org).

3 Jane Brown, *Gardens of a Golden Afternoon : The story of a partnership: Edwin Lutyens and* *Gertrude Jekyll* (Allen Lane, London, 1982), p.136.

4 *ibid.*

1 – 1925 reprint of map showing the outline of the lands at Inchicore North and Longmeadows in State ownership available for the proposed linear park, with a faint red cross indicating the proposed location of the Memorial Plot.
(National Archives of Ireland)

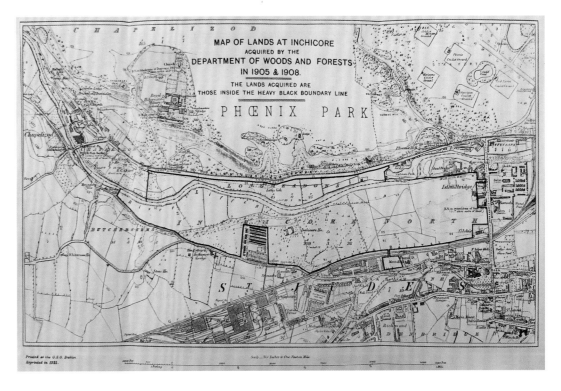

border decoration. He created seven designs: silhouettes of military scenes are mixed with drawings in black ink from Celtic mythology to form a setting for each page. However, a location and design for a permanent memorial to house these books was more difficult. Several proposals, including a monument in Merrion Square and a new commemorative entrance archway to the Phoenix Park, were considered, and then rejected, by the Free State government. In 1924 it was reported that 20,000 veterans and a crowd of 50,000 gathered at College Green for the 11th November Remembrance Day ceremony. From 1926 the Government granted permission to the British Legion (Irish Free State area) to erect a temporary cross beside the Wellington Monument in the Phoenix Park. Records show that ex-servicemen attended 11am mass at the Pro-Cathedral and then marched to the Phoenix Park for speeches and two minutes of silence. Each year the British Legion invited the President of the

Executive Council (the head of the Free State until 1937) to lay a wreath; the cabinet declined each year. By 1929 it was reported that the numbers attending the Remembrance Day ceremonies had dropped to about 10,000 ex-servicemen and a crowd of about 9,000. During the 1930s, the ceremonies attracted skirmishes with anti-Treaty forces (also known as the Irregulars), causing disturbances, and, following pressure from An Garda Síochána, the Government imposed restrictions on the sale of Flanders poppies, the display of the union flag and military-like marching. There was a growing awareness of a need for a suitable location for people to gather to mark Remembrance Day.

In 1929, Andrew Jameson, Memorial Committee, contacted WT Cosgrave, President of the Executive Council, to request that a portion of land in the Phoenix Park be allocated for a memorial. Cosgrave then asked the Office of Public Works for any suitable lands adjacent to the Phoenix Park. At a cabinet meeting on 29th September 1929, Thomas J Byrne, Principal Architect, OPW, presented a site to accommodate the annual Remembrance Day ceremonies. The National Archive records show a monumental park on part of the 'Long Meadows Estate West of St John's Road being that part opposite St Jude's Church, consisting in all of 25 acre[s] at present used for allotments with a square open space of nine acres with ceremonial roads and flowered margin with suitable monument of a wall type facing the park'.[5] The OPW drawing shows the main entrance to the Memorial Plot on the Inchicore Road, with a bridge across the Great Southern & Western Railway. The government approved this proposed site and promised extra funds for a public park.

I have found no record of the appointment of Edwin Lutyens or the brief for the INWMG.[6] However, Sir Dunbar Plunket Barton (chairman) and Andrew Jameson (treasurer) may have met Lutyens through his Irish clients and projects – Heywood Gardens, Co Laois (1906-12); Lambay Castle, Co Dublin (1905-12); Howth Castle, Co Dublin (1910-11) and his proposals for a Dublin art gallery for the Hugh Lane Collection (1912-13). Andrew Jameson was a collector of Irish art and a supporter of Hugh Lane's Dublin Art Gallery. In addition, Lutyens was particularly experienced in the design of war memorials and cemeteries and was at the peak of his career in 1929: his work at New Delhi was nearing completion (for which he received a knighthood) and he was appointed architect for Liverpool Cathedral. 'As the designer of our Memorial we selected Sir Edwin Lutyens, whom we are not alone in deeming the first architect of the age. His masterpieces are among the chief ornaments of Great Britain and of India, as well as of Ireland.'[7]

In 1930, Lutyens came to Ireland to inspect Longmeadows for the first time and meet WT Cosgrave, who was suitably impressed by his reputation. Lutyens prepared a design, which was forwarded to TJ Byrne, who compiled a lengthy report, and estimate of cost which he presented to Government the following year. Byrne's role was to be critical in the successful collaboration of this very sensitive project.

Thomas Joseph Byrne had much in common with Sir Edwin Lutyens,. Both were sons of military men; his Irish father was in the Royal Irish Fusiliers, his mother was English. He was brought up in Kingston, Surrey, and articled to a local architect for six years before moving to the office of Anthony Scott in Drogheda, where he worked alongside Scott's son William. Byrne returned to London in 1898 to complete his studies, and joined the Architects Department of the newly formed London County Council, which had a reputation for progressive work highly influenced by some of the leading practitioners of the Arts and Crafts Movement – Norman Shaw, William Lethaby, Charles Voysey and Philip Webb. In early 1901, Byrne moved back to Ireland to marry May Scott and take up a position at the South Dublin Rural District Council, with responsibility for the design and construction of Carnegie Libraries at Whitechurch and Clondalkin, labourers' cottages and private housing in Chapelizod. All were designed to the highest standards, meticulously detailed, and specified the use of local materials. Following the establishment of Dáil Éireann in 1919, WT Cosgrave initially appointed Byrne to the Local Government Board, then Acting Chief of the Local Government Housing Department, where he was influential in the development of housing policy. In a private capacity, Byrne designed the housing scheme at Mount Brown for Dublin Corporation, and the Bridge

---

5 National Archives of Ireland (NAI), TSCH/3/ S4156A, War Memorial, Selection of Site – map with red cross indicating proposed location for the memorial plot.

6 Unfortunately, the Lutyens Trust Archive has no

correspondence between Sir Edwin Lutyens and TJ Byrne or Andrew Jameson concerning the design and construction of the Irish National War Memorial at Islandbridge.

7 Sir Dunbar Plunket Barton speaking of the Memorial Executive Council, quoted in Lt Col

Boydell, 'The Irish National War Memorial: Its Meaning and Purpose' in British Legion Annual (Dublin, 1941), pp.15-51.

8 NAI, TSCH/3/S4156A, op. cit.

2 – Aerial view of the east end of
Longmeadows and North Inchicore,
with Kilmainham Gaol in the
foreground, 1918
(RAF photo / courtesy South Dublin Libraries)

Inn, Chapelizod; thus he may have been familiar with the lands at north Inchicore and Longmeadows.

When T J Byrne was appointed OPW Principal Architect in 1923, he started the mammoth task of rebuilding and restoring the General Post Office (GPO), the Customs House and the Four Courts, as well as the very many state buildings damaged during the War of Independence and Civil War, including a programme of National Schools and the conversion of RIC barracks to Garda stations.

Byrne reported on Sir Edwin Lutyens' design for the Irish National War Memorial on 14th December 1931.[8] He was clearly an admirer of Lutyens:

> the drawings and model now presented are ... the work
> of Sir Edwin Landseer Lutyens R.A. who may well be con-

sidered as among the greatest architects of today. His scheme has been produced after careful review of all the circumstances and close examination of the locality and of the advantages offered by the use of that tract of some 150 acres of riverside land, well varied in slope and aspect, along the south bank of the River Liffey which it is proposed, in effect, to add to Phoenix Park.'

Byrne describes the context for the Memorial Plot located near the eastern end of a new 150 acre parkway

> which can be best realised by viewing it from the winding
> road which skirts the southern boundary of the Phoenix
> Park whence the nicely rolling tract beyond the placid
> stream seems to stand against the foothills of Dublin in
> the southern distance.

He includes Lutyens' description of the proposed Memorial in his report.

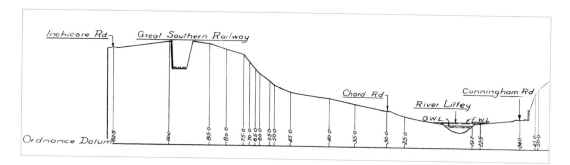

3 – Longitudinal section on the line
of the axis of Longmeadows Park
(OPW Library)

'I propose to confine the War Memorial to the area bounded by the circular road in the south and the river to the north, and about the centre of this site I place the great monolith Stone of Remembrance on a great lawn and behind it, to the south raised on the stairway leading to Inchicore Road, the cross – some thirty feet high. Flanking the War Stone are fountains which punctuate the diagonal vistas up to the Cross. To the east and west of the enclosed lawn, with its terraces, north and south are Pavilions for Name Records, connected by Pergolas which open into circular and terraced gardens.'

Byrne recommended Lutyens' design proposal to Government and it was approved. The Articles of Agreement between the Memorial Committee and the Minister of Finance of the Irish Free State were signed in 1933. The linear Public Park [Plate 1] was funded by Government, and the War Memorial by the Irish National War Memorial Trust. Sir Edwin Lutyens designed the main ceremonial entrance on Inchicore Road, with a new road between a colonnaded bridge over the railway lines leading onto the Horseshoe Road, bordering the ceremonial lawn and the symmetrical rose gardens. Lutyens created a strong central axis via a series of stepped terraces leading to the Memorial Cross – the Great War Stone – in the centre of the ceremonial lawn, and via the temple leading to a second bridge over the Liffey and Conyngham Road into the Phoenix Park.[9]

The first phase of this collaborative project was the laying out of the Public Park, which began in late 1931, and employed an equal number of ex-soldiers from both the British Army and the Irish

9 Interestingly, this strong axial line, which drops from the ridge at Inchicore Road down to the Liffey and up into the Phoenix Park, when extended, reaches Áras an Uachtaráin (formerly the Vice-Regal Lodge, residence of the Lord Lieutenant of Ireland), where the Memorial Committee was formed in 1919.

10 From Edwin Lutyens, 'Memorandum on the Graveyards of Battlefields' (1917) quoted in Colin Amery, Margaret Richardson and Gavin Stamp (eds.) Lutyens – The Work of the English Architect Sir Edwin Lutyens (1869-1944), catalogue of the retrospective exhibition at the Hayward Gallery, London in 1981-82 (Arts Council of Great Britain, 1981), p.150.

11 ibid.

12 ibid.

13 In architecture, entasis is the application of a convex curve to a surface for aesthetic purposes. Its best-known use is in certain orders of classical columns that curve slightly as their diameter is decreased from the bottom upwards.

14 When Lutyens visited the Western Front in 1917, he sketched a design for a cemetery in Trouville based on the plan of a cathedral with rows of trees in place of columns. Although never executed, it remained an ideal image for his later cemetery and monument designs. See Jeroen Geurst, Cemeteries of the Great War by Sir Edwin Lutyens (010 Publishers, Rotterdam, 2010), p.37.

15 See Plate 3, 'Longitudinal Section on the line of the axis of Longmeadows Park' for the location of Chord Road.

16 Today there is a National Day of Commemoration at the INWMG on the Sunday closest to 11th July and on the Sunday closest to 11th November, and Remembrance Sunday is marked by a ceremony in St Patrick's Cathedral, attended by the President of Ireland.

Army. Landscaping works included the filling of old gravel pits, converting cart tracks into metalled roads, reducing steep slopes and hollows, and making new entrances at Islandbridge and Chapelizod. Government-funding was drawn from the budget allocated to unemployment relief works, designed to tide over agricultural workers during the winter and to slow down migration.

In late 1933 the levelling and regrading of the north-facing Liffey valley started in preparation for the construction of the War Memorial. A longitudinal section drawing [Plate 3] on the line of the axis of Longmeadows Park indicates the extensive excavation and backfilling, which was done without mechanical excavators, to create the large flat central lawn and the flanking gardens. Furthermore, most of the construction work was carried out by hand; the only mechanical tools used were a steamroller, two cement mixers and a rope and pulley to lift the stone.

Edwin Lutyens' original, finely honed detailed design drawings for the Memorial exemplify his understanding of craft and demonstrate his extensive collaborative experience on country house garden projects and cemeteries with Gertrude Jekyll. Full-size drawings of stone details were converted into zinc templates by the resident engineer, Capt D Campbell, for the masons to shape, chisel and carve (by hand) granite from quarries at Ballyknockan, Co Wicklow, and Barnaculla, Co Dublin. The recent (2020) removal of two stones from one of the circular fountains (to investigate the internal drainage system) illustrates the complexity of carving three-dimensional curved and neatly interlocking segments, cut without the aid of machines or computers.

In 1917 Lutyens recommended that each cemetery and memorial, whether in Europe, Asia or Africa, should have one large, non-denominational monument and that it should be known as the Great War Stone. He strongly believed that the structure should be 'for all time ... and for men of all creeds',[10] and that they were 'all equally deserving enduring record'.[11] He specified that the stone should in all cases be selected from a local quarry and that

it should take 'the form of ONE great fair stone of fine proportions', 12ft long.[12] Edwin Lutyens designed the Great War Stone with entasis, so that there is no perfectly flat surface or straight line (he did this at the Cenotaph in London too).[13] The horizontal surface is spherical, and all the vertical lines converge upwards to a centre point 1801ft 8in above the spheres. A huge circle had to be set out (possibly in a large field or parade ground) so that a template could be made of a segment of the circle for the masons to hone each Great War Stone by hand. Lutyens stipulated that each Great War Stone was raised on a plinth of three steps, of which the first and third steps were to be twice the width of the second to accommodate the laying of wreaths. Lutyens intended that the Great War Stones would act as the focus of the cemetery or memorial in a vast cathedral-scale plan, whose vaulted ceiling is the sky.[14] Lutyens was working on his last great commission, the Catholic Cathedral in Liverpool, while designing INWMG. The central lawn at the INWMG is enclosed with retaining walls, pergolas and trees, lending a sense of the interior of a vast building; it resembles a theatrical stage, with an audience on the slope above, observing the Remembrance Day ceremony.

In 1935 Lutyens inspected the works and was pleased with what had been accomplished under the weekly supervision of T J Byrne, who visited the site every Saturday for the five years of the construction period. Works ceased in February 1938 when funding for the Memorial ran out, before the project was complete. Thus the main entrance at the junction of Inchicore Road and Memorial Road, the granite colonnaded bridge over the Great Southern Railway, the temple at the junction of the main axis and Chord Road,[15] and the masonry bridge across the Liffey all had to be omitted. Even so, the Memorial Gardens were not open to the public or used for a Remembrance Day ceremony. Under pressure from the British Legion, a formal opening was eventually agreed to for 30th July 1939, although rumours of war caused de Valera to abandon this planned event. Remembrance Day ceremonies finally took place in the Irish National War Memorial

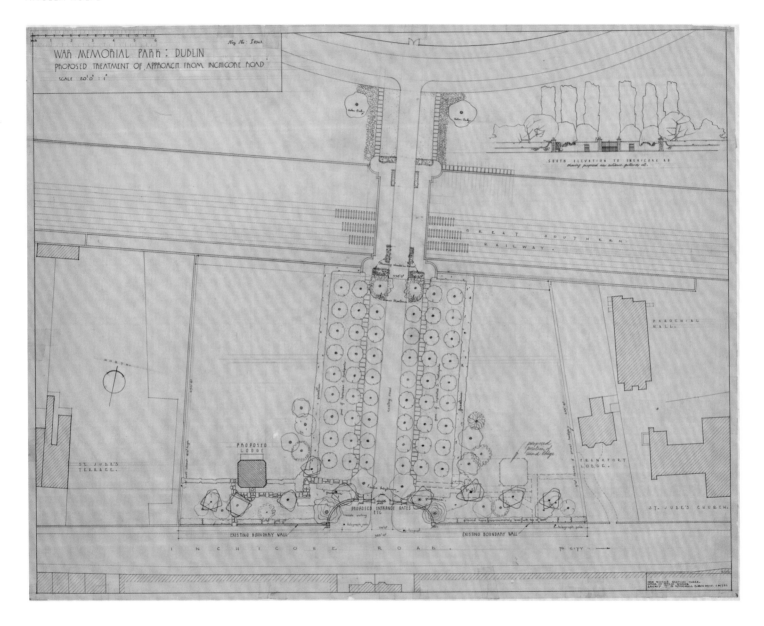

4 – *War Memorial Park – proposed treatment of*
approach from Inchicore Road, 1949-50
(OPW Library)

Gardens in 1940, and continued annually until 1970.[16] In 1941 the British Legion produced a publication, *The Irish National War Memorial: Its Meaning and Purpose*, by Lt. Col. Boydell as a permanent reminder of the splendour of Irish valour and the visible expression of our unparalleled national unity. It documents the process and emphasises the collaboration between the State and the Memorial Committee, and pays tribute to all those who participated to the realisation of the Memorial over nineteen years. The Memorial is a permanent witness to their 'earnest and indefatigable labours'.[17]

In 1949-50, the OPW produced a modified design for the completion of Lutyens' original design, but less elaborate. It included the ceremonial entrance on Inchicore Road, the railway bridge, two lodges for constables, and a public shelter and lavatory accommodation [Plate 4]. The OPW architects' proposal included double gates and a pair of pedestrian gates set in a rubble stone wall on the Inchicore Road, and the Memorial Road was to be flanked by a grove of cypress trees. But in 1953 the OPW was notified that a new road, connecting Ballyfermot to the city centre, was being contemplated by Dublin Corporation. So, when the road was built, only a simplified railway bridge and Memorial Road were constructed [Plate 5]. In 1955, the OPW gave a 99-year lease to Dublin Corporation on a section of the linear park, west of the Memorial plot, to develop as a public park. However, OPW files reveal that by 1969 the main access to the Memorial would be from the South Circular Road, Islandbridge,[18] where the OPW had to purchase a narrow strip of land from Dublin Corporation – adjacent to the flats that were under construction – for a new road. In the 1970s, the two plots on Memorial Road and Inchicore Road were subsequently developed as data centres for the Revenue Commissioners. In 1971 there was political pressure to develop a golf course in the linear park, which was not approved by the Minister for Finance.

In the mid-1980s there was a renewed interest in the contested period of Irish history from 1913 to 1923. A new Committee of Trustees of the Irish National War Memorial was appointed and negotiations with the OPW were entered into to restore the War Memorial. The IRA bombing of the Remembrance Day service at Enniskillen in 1987 may have had a significant impact on changing minds in relation to the all-Ireland National Memorial, located in Dublin. The restored Irish National War Memorial Gardens were finally formally opened in 1988, with tight security but no-one to represent the Irish government, and low-key remembrance ceremonies recommenced.

A further detrimental impact on the integrity of Lutyens' vision for a ceremonial entrance to the INWMG on Inchicore Road occurred in the 1980s when the Chapelizod bypass was constructed, removing any possibility for completing his original design. The dual-carriageway required road-widening and the construction of a reinforced concrete retaining wall that sliced off the top of the Horseshoe Road that encircles the War Memorial Gardens, altering the axial stairway behind the cross. Furthermore, it excluded Memorial Road from the Memorial Gardens and made the proposed formal entrance on Inchicore Road redundant. Today, access to the INWMG for residents of Kilmainham and Inchicore is via an inadequate pavement on the far side of a very busy national road, past second-rate pseudo gates and down a mean-spirited utilitarian ramp, which further isolates the Gardens from the community. It was interesting to note that, between March and June 2020, traffic noise and air pollution that had undermined the tranquillity of the Gardens disappeared and it was possible to cross the roads with ease, unimpeded by the constant stream of speeding vehicles or stop lights.

In 1994 Minister of Finance, Bertie Ahern, unveiled a replica temple on the main north-south axis. Sadly, it was constructed using reconstituted stone and a fibre-glass dome.

The War Memorial is expertly maintained by OPW staff and is

---

17 Boydell, 'Irish National War Memorial', p.12.
18 OPW, P5.35/4, S.43/1/49.

5 – Aerial view of INWMG showing road to Ballyfermot under construction, 1956
(National Library of Ireland / Morgan Aerial Photographic Collection)

greatly appreciated by the local community. The long process of reconciliation with this memorial was acknowledged in 2006 when for the first time a taoiseach attended a ceremony at the INWMG to commemorate the Irish war dead and in 2011 when President Mary McAleese brought Queen Elizabeth II to the Memorial Gardens.

The Irish National War Memorial was the last memorial designed by the architect Sir Edwin Lutyens. It represents a synthesis and apogee of Lutyens' lifetime's work, incorporating elements of Lutyens' poetic vision, rooted in the Arts and Crafts Movement and exhibited in the use of local materials, quality craftsmanship and beautiful planting. The layout and built structures are inspired by a logical classicism which he had employed in large country houses and public buildings, expressed in the formality of symmetry of the layout of New Delhi, and the empathy and humanism in the careful dignity of cemeteries which demonstrated his response to the chaos and suffering he had witnessed when he visited the Western Front in 1917.

2019 marked the 150th anniversary of the birth of Sir Edwin Lutyens. The OPW organised an international architectural competition for the design of a new bridge to acknowledge Lutyens' original design intention.[19] I was invited to prepare a temporary

[19] https://www.riai.ie/whats-on/news/announcement_of_winning_architect_to_design_new_bridge_at_islandbridge.

[20] The original site area outlined in the presentation to Government in 1929 was nine acres. However, the Lutyens design approved in 1931 covered 15 acres.

[21] https://architecturefoundation.ie/news/free-space-manifesto-biennale-architettura-2018/.

exhibition on the life and work of Lutyens for display in the Gardens. It gave me a wonderful opportunity to study a wealth of published information and to delve into files and study drawings to learn more about the process and context that enabled the INWMG to be constructed in the early years of the Irish Free State. I have been surprised to discover the high level of participation in the Remembrance Day activities up until 1939 and the considerable goodwill for the Memorial from both of the first two presidents of the Executive Council, WT Cosgrave and Éamon de Valera. Furthermore, I have been astonished at the level of ambition that has been demonstrated by the fact that the plan approved in 1931 was for a 15-acre memorial plot within a 150-acre linear public park to be linked to and eventually amalgamated into the Phoenix Park.[20] I have been humbled by the care and craftmanship demonstrated in the physical form, zeal and commitment of everyone involved in this extraordinary collaborative human endeavour achieved during turbulent times.

It would be marvellous if the original plan approved by Government in 1931 for a public park on the lands formally known as Longmeadows and North Inchicore [Plate 6] and linked by an accessible pedestrian bridge to the Phoenix Park could be fully realised before the centenary of that far-sighted decision. Furthermore, consideration would need to be given to traffic-calming and a 'green bridge' on Memorial Road and Con Colbert Road to improve safety and the environment for pedestrians entering the INWMG from Inchicore Road, as proposed in a joint OPW/DCC architectural competition held in 2007.

The INWMG perfectly aligns with Grafton Architect's FREE-SPACE manifesto for the Biennale Architettura 2018, which describes a generosity of spirit and a sense of humanity at the core of architecture's agenda, focusing on the quality of space itself,[21] and quotes a Greek proverb: 'A society grows great when old men plant trees whose shade they know they shall never sit in.'

6 – View of the INWMG with the extent of the 1933 proposed linear public park outlined in red (Google, 2021)

Stone seat detail • February

Stone steps • August

Rose garden • January

Rose garden • July

Book rooms • May

Suggested reading

Colin Amery + Margaret Richardson, *Lutyens: The Work of the English Architect Sir Edwin Lutyens (1869-1944),* Hayward Gallery catalogue (Arts Council of Great Britain, 1981)

Síghle Bhreathach-Lynch, 'Political Sculpture in 20th Century Dublin: art as a barometer of political expression in visualizing Dublin', in Justin Carville (ed.), *Visualizing Dublin: visual culture, modernity and the representation of urban space* (Peter Lang AG, Bern, 2014)

Jane Brown, *Gardens of a Golden Afternoon: The Story of a Partnership – Edwin Lutyens & Gertrude Jekyll* (Allen Lane, London, 1982)

John Byrne + Michael Fewer, *Thomas Joseph Byrne, Nation Builder* (South County Dublin Council, 2013)

HB Clarke, *Irish Historic Towns Atlas no. 11 – Dublin, part I, to 1610* (Royal Irish Academy, Dublin, 2002).

Jane Clarke, *All the Way Home* (Smith|Doorstop Books, Sheffield, 2019) (poems inspired by WWI letters in the Auerbach Family Archive)

Fergus A D'Arcy, *Remembering the War Dead: British Commonwealth and International War Graves in Ireland since 1914* (Office of Public Works, Trim, 2007)

Dublin City Archive, Monica Roberts Collection, Royal Dublin Fusiliers Association Archives, https://repository.dri.ie/catalog/v9807j056 (letters from Irish soldiers at the Front to Ms Roberts, 1914-18)

Dublin City Archive, ref. INWM/002/01/01-213, Minutes of Irish National War Memorial Management Committee, 1937-1996

Fionnuala Fallon, 'Garden of Tranquility', *The Irish Times,* 16th August 2014; https://www.irishtimes.com/life-and-style/homes-and-property/gardens/garden-of-tranquility-1.1893687

Jeroen Geurst, *Cemeteries of the Great War by Sir Edwin Lutyens* (010 Publishers, Rotterdam, 2010)

Stephen H Harrison and Raghnall Ó Floinn, *Viking Graves and Grave-Goods in Ireland,* Medieval Dublin Excavations, 1962-81, Ser B, 11 (National Museum of Ireland, Dublin, 2014)

Marguerite Helmers, *Harry Clarke's War: illustrations for Ireland's memorial records, 1914-1918* (Irish Academic Press, Dublin, 2016)

John Horne + Edward Madigan (eds), *Towards Commemoration: Ireland in War and Revolution 1912-1923* (Royal Irish Academy, Dublin, 2013)

Gertrude Jekyll + Lawrence Weaver, *Gardens of Small Country Houses* (*Country Life,* 1911 / Macmillan, London, 1983)

Ruth Johnson, *Viking Age Dublin* (Vermillion, Dublin, 2014)

Peter Neill (ed.), *For Evermore: Fading Evidence of the Great War* (Gallery of Photography, Dublin, 2000)

OPW, 'The Irish National War Memorial Gardens, Conservation Management Plan', consultation draft, March 2016, http://phoenixpark.ie/wp-content/uploads/2017/08/WM-CMP-PDF.compressed-1.pdf

Carole Pollard 'Case Study: Irish National War Memorial Gardens, Islandbridge, Dublin 8 1939', in Ellen Rowley (ed.), *More than Concrete Blocks: Dublin city's twentieth-century buildings and their stories,* Vol. 1, 1900-40 (Dublin City Council, 2016)

Seán Rothery, *Ireland and the New Architecture 1900-1940* (Lilliput Press, Dublin, 1991)

Tim Skelton + Gerald Gliddon, *Lutyens and the Great War* (Frances Lincoln Publishers, London, 2008)

Yvonne Whelan, *Reinventing Modern Dublin: streetscape, iconography and politics of identity* (UCD Press, Dublin, 2003)

_____

Further information:

http://opwdublincommemorative.ie/war-memorial/

https://heritageireland.ie/places-to-visit/irish-national-war-memorial-gardens/

Contributors

ANNIE DIBBLE spent her formative years in Surrey, England. Her maternal grandparents were from Co Tyrone and her father's parents were both English. Young men from both families fought in two world wars. Her Irish grandparents were also photographers; the albums she pored over as a child shared visual evidence of military history, while war stories were dinner table conversations. After studying Art and Design in Manchester, Annie moved to Ireland, and has since travelled widely with her camera, researching indigenous textiles to support her role as a lecturer in textile design at NCAD, Dublin. She researched and co-produced *Tana Bana* (2015) with director Pat Murphy, a documentary film on silk zari-weavers in Varanasi, India, and has just completed writing a book on the subject. Annie has lived a three-minute walk from the Memorial Gardens in Dublin since 1980.

ANGELA ROLFE completed her architectural education in UCD two years after her move to Ireland in 1975, and a Masters in Urban Design in 2006. She served as an architect in the Office of Public Works between 1980 and 2017, where she was responsible for the restoration, adaptation, upgrading and maintenance of a broad range of state property, including Dublin Castle, Government Buildings and Áras an Uachtaráin. She is currently chair of the RIAI Universal Design Task Force, deputy director of UIA Architecture for All Work Programme, member of RIAI International Affairs Committee, Save Kilmainham Mill Group, Kilmainham Inchicore Network, Inchicore Regeneration Consultative Forum and part-time lecturer at the Yeats Academy of Art, Design and Architecture, IT Sligo. Angela has lived on Inchicore Road since 1977.

ELAINE SISSON is a cultural historian and Senior Lecturer at the Creative Futures Academy, IADT. She completed an MA at the College of William and Mary in Virginia, and a PhD at Trinity College, Dublin. She has broadcast and published widely on Irish culture of the late 19th and early 20th particularly in relation to popular culture, theatre, film, performance and Irish modernism. She has lived in Kilmainham for twenty years.

FIONNUALA WALDRON is Professor Emerita and Cregan Professor of Education at Dublin City University. She began her career as a primary teacher, joining the staff of St Patrick's College, DCU, in 1999, where she specialised in history education and global citizenship education. In 2005, she founded the Centre for Human Rights and Citizenship Education which focuses on applied research in areas such as human rights education and climate change education. Fionnuala has a range of publications across the fields of history and education.

RUTH JOHNSON is City Archaeologist with Dublin City Council since 2001. A graduate of the Institute of Archaeology, University College London, she has a PhD in Medieval History from Trinity College Dublin. She is the author of several academic and popular books, articles and exhibitions on the history and archaeology of Viking age, medieval and later Dublin. She is a resident of Inchicore, where she lives with her husband and their two children in the CIÉ estate.

MAEVE O'SULLIVAN is from Dún Laoghaire and teaches in further education in Dublin. Her poetry and haiku have been widely published, awarded, anthologised and translated. She is the author of five collections from Alba Publishing (UK) – *Initial Response* (2011), *Vocal Chords* (2014), *A Train Hurtles West* (2015), *Elsewhere* (2017) and *Wasp on the Prayer Flag* (2021). Maeve leads workshops and mentors individuals in haiku (www.maeveosullivan.com).

Capt (Retd) GALE A SCANLAN AIIRSM is from Co Tyrone. She graduated from the University of Ulster in English and Theatre Studies. She attended the Royal Military Academy Sandhurst and received the Queen's Commission in 1988. She served with the Royal Military Police in the UK, Northern Ireland, Germany and Hong Kong until 1997. Gale completed a Masters in Cultural Policy and Arts Management at UCD in 1998. She is now Head of Operations at the Irish Museum of Modern Art in the Royal

Hospital Kilmainham, and has been on the Board of Trustees of the INWMG since 2007.

ANNE TANNAM is a Dublin poet with three collections of poetry published to date – *Take This Life* (Wordonthestreet, 2011), *Tides Shifting Across My Sitting Room Floor* (Salmon Poetry, 2017) and *Twenty-six Letters of a New Alphabet* (Salmon Poetry, 2021). For more information on Anne's poetry, visit www.annetannampoetry.ie.

ANNEMARIE NÍ CHURREÁIN is a poet from the Donegal gaeltacht. Her publications include *Bloodroot* (Doire Press, 2017) and *Town* (Salvage Press, 2018). Her work has been shortlisted for the Shine Strong Award for best first collection in Ireland. Ní Churreáin is a recipient of the Next Generation Artist Award from the Arts Council / An Chomhairle Ealaíon and a co-recipient of the inaugural Markievicz Award. In 2020, she was an artist-in-residence at the Centre Culturel Irlandais, Paris. For more information visit www.studiotwentyfive.com.

JEAN O'BRIEN's *Fish on a Bicycle: New & Selected Poems* (Salmon Poetry, 2016) is her fifth collection. Her work has received awards from Arvon International and the Fish Poetry Prize, and was also highly placed in the Forward Prize and Voices of War. She was awarded the Kavanagh Fellowship in 2017/18. Jean holds an M.Phil from Trinity College, Dublin, tutors in creative writing and poetry, and is currently working on a sixth collection due to be published by Salmon Poetry in autumn 2021.

SHEILA GORMAN explores military themes through words and painting. Her Masters in Art History (NCAD, 1991) focused on 'Aspects of the Psychology and Sociology of Uniforms of the British Military with particular reference to the Royal Irish Fusiliers in the Great War'. Her stories have been broadcast by RTÉ and BBC, and published by *Crannóg* magazine and *New Irish Writing*. Sheila worked in the Douglas Hyde Gallery Before joining the Arts Council Department of Human Resources in 1996. She exhibits her paintings and holds an MA in Screenwriting (IADT, 2003).

RITA DUFFY is one of Ireland's groundbreaking visual artists, exhibiting in Ireland and internationally, initiating major collaborative art projects with architects, poets and communities, visiting lecturer at international universities, with contributions to numerous publications and media engagements. Based on the Cavan/Fermanagh border in a former courthouse, she continues to explore issues of female identity, history and politics, working in this specific 'neither here nor there place'. In 2018 she was recognised for her contribution to visual arts in Ireland and elected to Aosdána. Duffy's work is held in museums and private collections worldwide, and her public art projects continue to grow in scale and ambition

NUALA HAYES is an actor, storyteller and independent broadcaster who has lived with her family in Dublin 8 since 1976, and in Islandbridge beside the Liffey since 1990. She has collected stories from many parts of Ireland, including Cape Clear Island in Co Cork, and Laois and Offaly, and is the author of *Laois Folktales* (History Press Ireland, 2015). She is currently chairperson of Storytellers of Ireland, a voluntary organisation dedicated to the perpetuation of storytelling in all its forms (www.strorytellersofireland.com).

THIS BOOK IS DEDICATED TO ALL THOSE WHO DIED TOO SOON

Acknowledgements

We would like to thank the members of the Irish National War Memorial Trust who in their role as custodians of the Irish National War Memorial Gardens have given their full support for the publication of this book.

Our gratitude goes to
— the Commemorations Unit of the Department of Tourism, Culture, Arts, Gaeltacht, Sport & Media for funding *Shadows and Reflections*.
— Mary Shine Thompson, Nuala Hayes, Art Ó Briain, Fionnuala Waldron, Peter O'Loughlin, whose enthusiastic responses provided the initial encouragement to move this project forward.
— To Edward Burke and Helen O'Donoghue for making connections, and Marcus Collier for local information on bats and time capsules.
— Dublin City Archives and the National Archives for pointing us in the right direction.
— The National Library, National Museum, South County Dublin Libraries and the Office of Public Works Library for making images available during Covid pandemic restrictions.
— Kevin McCarthy, Executive Assistant to the President
— The Lutyens Trust
— The Irish Craft Writers Group for their critical feedback.
— Fionnuala Fallon for the flowers

— All Office of Public Works staff whose commitment and dedication has continued the legacy of TJ Byrne, Edwin Lutyens and Gertrude Jeykell through maintaining, planting, restoring and tending the Irish National War Memorial Gardens for the last eighty years — thank you!

Last, but not least, our heartfelt thanks to the contributing poets and essayists who have so enthusiastically shared their often deeply personal reflections on the Irish National War Memorial Gardens and what it means for them.

———

a doubling of deaths   the wisteria buds fatter

— Maeve O'Sullivan

Chronology

1914 – Local World War I recruits assemble at Richmond Barracks

1915 – Royal Irish Regimen leave Inchicore for Rouen

1916 – Richmond Barracks, Inchicore, becomes holding centre for rebels during the Easter Rising.
 – Signatories of the Proclamation sent to Kilmainham Gaol for execution
 – Tom Kettle, Irish poet and Parliamentary Party MP, killed in action during the Somme offensive

1917 – Frances Ledwidge, Irish war poet and trade unionist, killed at Paschendale on 31st July

1918 – Royal Air Force aerial photograph of Kilmainham and surrounding areas
 – First meeting of the Memorial Committee in Ireland to raise funds

1920 – Military barricades and cordons erected in Inchicore and other roads into Dublin
 – 400 raids on businesses and homes in Rialto, South Circular Road, Inchicore Railway Works, Kilmainham and Goldenbridge carried out by British military and auxiliary police in one day
 – Railway workers refuse to handle munitions trains or trains carrying military forces

1921 – Inchicore cinema opens
 – Ernie O'Malley, Simon Donnelly and Frank Teeling escape from Kilmainham Gaol on orders from Michael Collins

World War I | Irish War of Independence

This chronological account of events has been designed to place the Irish National War Memorial Gardens in a local and national historical context. Significant events between 1914 and 2020 have been selected to give a broader perspective and background to the development and role of the Memorial Gardens in Irish life. The Memorial Gardens are a repository of cultural memory and history that provides continuity and gives a sense of place. It is inevitable that there will be some anomalies and omissions in the selection of events, but it is hoped that this multifaceted chronology will bring texture, depth, fresh insight and a greater understanding of the meaning and significance of the Irish National War Memorial Gardens – a moment to acknowledge the shadows while reflecting on its beauty and endurance.

1914 – World War I begins 4th August

1915 – Irish Divisions suffers heavy losses at Gallipoli
 – Pope Benedict demands withdrawal of Irish support for World War I

1916 – Easter Rising, Dublin
 – 5,500 die in the Battle of the Somme (in which twenty Irish battalions took part)

1917 – Edwin Lutyens designs the War Stone for the Imperial War Graves Commission

1918 – General election in Britain and Ireland
 – First Dáil Éireann convened at the Mansion House, Dublin
 – General strike against conscription
 – Armistice declared 11th November
 – Spanish flu pandemic takes hold in Ireland

1919 – Declaration of Independence in January marks the start of the War of Independence
 – Treaty of Versailles signed in July

1920 – Cenotaph at Whitehall, London, designed by Edwin Lutyens
 – Unknown soldier interred at Westminster Abbey
 – British solders kill fourteen spectators at Croke Park, Dublin (Bloody Sunday)
 – Burning of Cork city by British forces
 – Government of Ireland Act (1920) establishes separate parliaments in Ireland, north and south
 – Spanish flu pandemic ends: 23,000 deaths in Ireland

1921 – Northern Ireland parliament opens
 – Custom House, Dublin, burnt down by the IRA
 – Second Dáil Éireann convened at the Mansion House, Dublin
 – Anglo-Irish Treaty signed in December

1922 – Richmond Barracks and Islandbridge Barracks taken over by the Free State Army
– Royal Hospital Kilmainham (RHK) evacuated by the British Army
– Kilmainham Gaol used as a military prison by the Free State Army during the Civil War

1923 – *Ireland's Memorial Records* published
– Yeats and Gogarty gift a pair of swans to the River Liffey following Gogarty's swim to safety escaping from the IRA
– 90 female Republican prisoners in Kilmainham Gaol end their hunger strike

1924 – 70,000 people mark Armistice Day at College Green, Dublin
– Former Kilmainham Sessions House reopened as Kilmainham Courthouse

1925 – Shots and smoke bombs interrupt two-minutes silence at Armistice Day ceremonies in Phoenix Park

1926 – Government allows the British Legion to erect a temporary cross in the Phoenix Park for the Armistice Day ceremony

1927 – British Legion Hall for employees of Great Southern Railway employees burnt down five days after opening
– RHK ceases to be used as a home for elderly soldiers

1928 – Armistice Day ceremonies held in Phoenix Park

1929 – Longmeadows site at Islandbridge agreed for the Irish National War Memorial Gardens (INWMG)
– Statutory order closing Kilmainham Gaol

1930 – Sir Edwin Lutyens visits the site at Longmeadows and meets WT Cosgrave.
– Grotto of Lourdes at Oblates' Church, Inchicore, constructed
– RHK used as Garda HQ until 1950

1931 – Sir Edwin Lutyens design for the INWMG approved by the Memorial Committee and Council of State, 14th December
– Last trams completed at Spa Road Works, Inchicore

1932 – Armistice Day ceremonies held in the Phoenix Park (sale of Flanders poppies restricted to two days)
– University College Dublin Boat Club established on the north side of the Liffey

1933 – Articles of Agreement between the Minister for Finance of Saorstát Éireann and NWM Trust signed
– Five pagan and eight Christian graves found during construction
– St Michael's parish church established

1934 – Viking warrior skeleton discovered on site; displayed at National Museum
– Tyrconnell Road housing developed by Dublin Utility Society

---

Irish Civil War	1920s	early 1930s

1922 – Dáil Éireann approves Anglo-Irish Treaty
– Anti-Treaty group form Cumann na Poblachta
– Irish Free State (Agreement) Act gives force to the Treaty
– *Ulysses,* by James Joyce, published

1923 – First performance of Seán O'Casey's *The Shadow of a Gunman* at the Abbey Theatre
– End of Civil War in Ireland
– William Butler Yeats is the first Irish person to win the Nobel Prize for Literature
– Censorship of Films Act (1923) introduced
– Prison ship *Argenta* holding 732 Catholic men in Belfast Lough

1924 – Irish Boundary Commission established

1925 – Dublin Metropolitan Police (DMP) amalgamated with An Garda Síochána

1926 – General strike in Great Britain
– Éamon de Valera inaugurates the Fianna Fáil party
– George Bernard Shaw awarded Nobel Prize for Literature

1927 – General election in Free State; WT Cosgrave re-elected President of Executive Council

1928 – New Free State currency issued

1929 – Shannon Hydroelectric power station at Ardnacrusha completed

1930 – Irish Free State elected to the Council of the League of Nations
– Restoration of the Custom House completed by TJ Byrne (OPW Principal Architect)

1931 – *Irish Press* newspaper founded by Éamon de Valera
– All India Gate Memorial, New Delhi, designed by Edwin Lutyens, commemorates 70,000 Indians who died in World War I

1932 – 31st Eucharistic Congress held in Dublin
– Northern Ireland's parliament buildings at Stormont open
– Memorial to the Missing of the Somme at Thiepval, designed by Lutyens, unveiled
– Rebuilding of GPO on O'Connell Street completed by TJ Byrne.

1933 – Éamon de Valera re-elected President of the Executive Council in general election

1934 – Rebuilding of Four Courts completed by TJ Byrne

1935 – Sir Edwin Lutyens visits the site at Longmeadows to view progress

1936 – On Armistice Day, all flags banned at Phoenix Park Remembrance Day event

1937 – Request to hold Remembrance Day Ceremony in the Memorial Gardens instead of the Phoenix Park refused (held in the Phoenix Park annually until 1941)

1938 – Completion certificate signed by Lutyens and TJ Byrne for the construction of the Irish National War Memorial Gardens
– Kilmainham Garda Station moves from Emmet Road to Kilmainham Lane

1939 – TJ Byrne, OPW Principal Architect and supervising architect for INWMG, dies
– Scheduled formal opening ceremony for INWM cancelled
– Armistice Day ceremonies take place in the Phoenix Park as usual

1940 – Government gives permission for first annual Remembrance Day ceremonies held at INWMG with restricted numbers

1941 – British Legion publishes a pamphlet, *The Irish National War Memorial, Its Meaning and Purpose*
– Rosary Novena at Inchicore Grotto attended by300,000

1942 – Remembrance Day ceremonies held annually at the INWMG until 1969
– Islandbridge Barracks renamed Clancy Barracks
– Commercial Rowing Club moves from Ringsend to the north side of the Liffey

1944 – Civil Service Hurling Club is established at Islandbridge

1946 – Trustees seek advice from OPW about the advisability of opening the Memorial Park to the public without permits in future

1947 – Nationalised transport company, Córas Iompair Éireann (CIÉ), introduces major changes at Inchicore Railway Works

1949 – OPW recommends necessary works required before the Memorial Park can be opened to the public

late 1930s	World War II	post-war years

1936 – Office of the Governor General abolished

1937 – New constitution for Irish Free State approved by Dáil Éireann

1938 – Anglo-Irish Agreements on Treaty ports, finance and trade ends the Economic War (1932-38) with the UK
– Douglas Hyde inaugurated as first President of Ireland

1939 – UK and France declare war on Germany and World War II begins in September
– Iveagh House is bequeathed to the State by the Earl of Iveagh

1940 – Government of Ireland introduces Emergency Powers (Amendment) Bill and Offences Against the State (Amendment) Bill to combat the IRA

1941 – German bombing of North Strand, Dublin
– USA enters the war following the Japanese bombing of Pearl Harbour

1942 – Irish ship rescues British and American survivors in north Atlantic
– Turf is stockpiled in the Phoenix Park

1943 – Irish ship rescues German naval survivors
– Two Irish merchant ships torpedoed by German U-boats in north Atlantic

1944 – British government bans all travel between Great Britain and Ireland

1945 – Séan T Kelly elected second President of Ireland

1946 – George Bernard Shaw awarded the Freedom of Dublin

1947 – United Nations Declaration of Human Rights adopted

1948 – John A Costello (Fine Gael) elected Taoiseach

1949 – Ireland leaves the Commonwealth on becoming a Republic
– Ireland becomes a founder member of the Council of Europe, accepting the jurisdiction of the European Court of Human Rights

1950 – Budget agreed to works required before the Park can be opened to the public

1953 – OPW notified by Dublin Corporation that the construction of a new roadway is being contemplated linking Ballyfermot with the city centre

1954 – Kilmainham Gaol designated a National Monument

1955 – Garda Boat Club established on the north side of the Liffey

1956 – Base of the Memorial Cross is damaged by a bomb placed by an IRA splinter group on 25th December (repair of damage: £30)

1957 – Construction of new road to Ballyfermot, cutting off proposed main entrance to the Memorial

1958 – Base of the Memorial Cross is again damaged by a bomb placed by an IRA splinter group on 25th December (repair of damage: £5)

1965 – Funeral of WT Cosgrave, first President of the Executive Council, at Goldenbridge Cemetery

1966 – OPW Chairman Harry Mundow suggests 'as a symbolic gesture of reconciliation' that the planned garden be completed and the planned bridge across the Liffey to the Phoenix Park be built

1967 – INWM Trustees and OPW agree that there 'is no scope for development of the entrance from the new Ballyfermot Road as a ceremonial entrance'

1969 – INWMG maintained by twelve OPW staff
     – Demolition of Keogh Square, formerly Richmond Barracks

1950s | **early 1960s** | **late 1960s**

1951 – Taoiseach Éamon de Valera visits Northern Ireland twice

1952 – Ireland excluded from Marshall Aid due to its wartime neutrality

1953 – Unemployment marches in Dublin
     – Sinn Féin decides to contest the next Westminster elections in Northern Ireland
     – Great Northern Railway sold to the governments of the Republic and Northern Ireland to be run jointly

1954 – Marian Year processions around Ireland
     – Renewal of IRA activity in Northern Ireland

1955 – Ireland admitted to the United Nations

1956 – IRA launches a border campaign in Northern Ireland

1957 – IRA members, north and south, arrested
     – Limerick WW1 Memorial and Gough Monument in the Phoenix Park blown up

1959 – Éamon de Valera becomes 3rd President of Ireland

1960 – Telefís Éireann, Irish national television service, established

1961 – John F Kennedy becomes the first US President of Irish Catholic descent

1962 – IRA calls off border campaign in Northern Ireland

1963 – President Kennedy visits Ireland
     – Assassination of President Kennedy, Dallas

1964 – Bridge over River Foyle linking Lifford and Strabane opens

1965 – State funeral of Roger Casement at Glasnevin Cemetery

1966 – 50th anniversary of Easter Rising
     – Garden of Remembrance at Parnell Square opened
     – Nelson's Pillar on Dublin's O'Connell Street blown up by IRA
     – Free secondary education scheme announced

1967 – Taoiseach Jack Lynch and NI Prime Minister Terence O'Neill meet for talks in Stormont

1968 – Taoiseach Jack Lynch and NI Prime Minister Terence O'Neill meet for talks in Dublin
     – First civil rights march in Northern Ireland

1969 – British troops arrive in Northern Ireland to 'back up the RUC'
     – Civil rights marches in Northern Ireland
     – NI Prime Minister Terence O'Neill resigns
     – Sectarian riots in Northern Ireland
     – US moon-landing

1970 – Remembrance Day ceremonies
transferred to St Patrick's Cathedral
– Completion of St Michael's Estate on the
site of Keogh Square / Richmond
Barracks, Inchicore
1972 – Dr John O'Connell TD arranges a
meeting between a leader of the
Provisional IRA and former Prime
Minister Harold Wilson at his home on
Inchicore Road

1979 – A million people celebrate mass on 29th
September in the Phoenix Park to
welcome Pope John-Paul II to Ireland
– Unexcavated earth moved from Dublin
Corporation's Wood Quay site to
Longmeadows where a Viking sword is
discovered by three local schoolboys
(now in the National Museum)

1980 – Elm trees on the Gardens' central avenue
and two shorter avenues succumb to
Dutch elm disease; replaced with lime
trees, birch and poplars
1981 – Concert at Longmeadows to raise funds
to build a new Gaelscoil
1982 – The INWMG listed by ICOMOS / IFLA
International Committee for Heritage
Gardens
1984 – Royal Hospital Kilmainham restored

| early 1970s | late 1970s | early 1980s |

1970 – Alliance Party formed in Northern Ireland
– Arms crisis in Republic of Ireland
1971 – Sale of Remembrance Day poppies
ceases in Republic of Ireland
– Decimalisation of currency introduced
– Death toll in the Troubles exceeds 100
1972 – Bloody Sunday in Derry and Bloody
Friday in Belfast
– British Embassy in Dublin burned in rioting
– Stormont parliament dissolved and direct
rule imposed in Northern Ireland
1973 – Ireland, UK and Denmark join the EEC
– Northern Ireland Assembly established
– Sunningdale Agreement signed
1974 – Ulster Workers' Council strike
– Guildford and Birmingham pub bombings
(Guildford 4 and Maguire 7 convicted)
– Dublin and Monaghan bombings
1975 – Ireland holds the Presidency of the
Council of the European Council for the
first time
– Three members of the Miami Showband
killed in an ambush in Co Down
– Tiede Herrema kidnap and siege in
Monasterevin, Co Kildare

1976 – British Ambassador to Ireland killed by
landmine in Sandyford, Co Dublin
– Ten Protestant workmen killed in
retaliation for killing of six Catholic
civilians (Kingsmill massacre)
– Death of three young children in
Northern Ireland leads to founding of NI
Peace Movement by their aunt Mairéad
Corrigan and Betty Williams (awarded
Nobel Peace Prize, 1976)
1977 – IRA bombing campaign in London
– Peace rally takes place in Belfast
– Queen Elizabeth II visits Northern Ireland
as part of her Silver Jubilee
1978 – European Court of Human Rights finds
Britain guilty of inhuman and degrading
treatment of republican internees in
Northern Ireland
1979 – Lord Mountbatten killed in IRA bombing
at Mullaghmore, Co Sligo
– Pope John Paul II pays three-day visit to
Ireland
– Ireland ends Irish pound parity with UK
pound sterling on joining the European
Monetary System

1981 – Bobby Sands goes on hunger strike in the
Maze Prison, wins UK by-election and
dies just weeks later on 8th May
– Hunger strikes end after 7 months and 10
deaths, leading to riots in Belfast and 120
injured in Dublin demonstration
– *Lutyens: the Work of the English architect Sir
Edwin Lutyens (1869-1944)* shown at the
Hayward Gallery, London
1982 – The first Ulster Assembly boycotted by
SDLP and Sinn Féin
– INLA kill 17 in bomb attack at the
Droppin' Well Inn, Ballykelly, Co Derry
1983 – 134 IRA prisoners escape from the Maze
Prison
– Shergar, the 1981 Derby winner, is
kidnapped; £2m ransom demanded, but
not paid (Shergar never found)
1984 – Consignment of IRA arms found on Irish
trawler off the SW coast
– New Ireland Forum report
– Four-day state visit by US President
Ronald Reagan

1985 – New INWMG Memorial Committee convened; INWMG designated Charitable Trust

1986 – First phase of restoration works complete
– INWM featured in a film on BBC TV

1987 – Phase 2 of restoration works comprising gates, railings, landscaping and tree surgery complete. INWMG now maintained by three OPW staff, reduced from twelve in the 1960s
– St Jude's Church demolished, leaving just the spire; stone reused to build the Steam Museum, Straffan, Co Kildare

1988 – INWMG refurbishment works complete.
– Gaelscoil Inse Chór primary school established in the park adjacent to the Memorial Gardens
– Irish Army hand over demilitarised Magazine Fort in Phoenix Park to OPW

1989 – Annual INWMG visitor numbers of 3,500 reported to Trustees
– Department of Finance withholds EEC Structural Funding for completion of Memorial as envisaged by Lutyens

1990 – 5,375 sign INWMG visitors' book
– OPW funding proposal for Liffey bridge rejected

1991 – Burmese teak 'Lutyens' seats replaced by hardwearing metal versions (originals donated to Leopardstown Park Hospital)
– Royal Hospital Kilmainham becomes the Irish Museum of Modern Art

1992 – The years 1939-1945 inscribed on the Great Cross to honour Irishmen killed in World War II

1993 – Alternative design for Lutyens' Temple completed
– OPW awarded the Incorporated Association of Architects & Surveyors' James Culleton Award for the restoration of the INWMG

1994 – Taoiseach Bertie Ahern declares open the replica Temple in the restored INWMG
– Conservation Volunteers Ireland (CVI) plant native species, mostly ash and birch, some oak, holly, hawthorn and blackthorn, as a visual buffer to the Chapelizod bypass

1995 – 75th anniversary of the Battle of the Somme service held at the INWMG in September

1996 – Oak sapling planted in memory of Capt Campbell Heather, Trustee of the INWM

1998 – Irish Army closes Clancy Barracks

---

late 1980s | **early 1990s** | **late 1990s**

1985 – Anglo-Irish Agreement signed in Belfast by Margaret Thatcher and Garret Fitzgerald
– Nine RUC killed in IRA attack in Newry

1986 – 30,000 emigrate to the USA
– Giant's Causeway designated Ireland's first UNESCO World Heritage Site

1987 – IRA bomb Remembrance Day, Enniskillen
– Eight IRA members die in an abortive attack on an RUC post at Loughgall

1988 – Sale of Remembrance Poppies resumed in the Republic of Ireland
– Milltown Cemetery attack by Loyalist kills three in Belfast; two British soldiers abducted and beaten to death at funerals of IRA members killed at cemetery
– National Archives of Ireland established
– Dublin celebrates 1,000 years since the first Viking settlement

1989 – Guildford 4 and Maguire 7 released
– 10,000 march to British Embassy in Dublin demanding British withdrawal from Northern Ireland

1990 – Mary Robinson elected President of Ireland
– Somme Association established in Northern Ireland
– Ireland holds Presidency of the EEC

1991 – Convictions of the Maguire Seven and Birmingham Six quashed
– Dublin inaugurated as European Capital of Culture

1992 – Mary Robinson is first President of Ireland to visit Belfast
– Royal Munster Fusiliers Association formed

1993 – IRA bomb kills 2 children in Warrington, UK
– IRA bomb a fish shop on the Shankill Road, Belfast, killing 10
– UDA shoot 21 in rising Sun bar in Greysteel, Co Derry
– President Robinson attends Remembrance Day service in St Patrick's Cathedral, Dublin

1994 – Provisional IRA announces a complete cessation of military operations
– Historic meeting between Albert Reynolds, John Hume and Gerry Adams at Government Buildings in Dublin
– Loyalist paramilitary groups announce ceasefire

– Inaugural session of the Forum for Peace and Reconciliation, Dublin Castle

1995 – Ireland v England soccer match abandoned when English supporters riot

1996 – Mary Robinson is first President of Ireland to visit Queen Elizabeth II in the UK
– IRA bomb in London Docklands

1997 – Mary McAleese inaugurated as 8th President of Ireland
– Royal Dublin Fusiliers Association formed

1998 – Good Friday Agreement is endorsed by referenda north and south of the border
– Island of Ireland Peace Tower at Messines unveiled by President McAleese, Queen Elizabeth II and King Albert II of Belgium
– 29 killed in terrorist bomb in Omagh
– US President Clinton visits Ireland

1999 – Senator George Mitchell Peace Bridge opened on the Cavan-Fermanagh border
– First meeting of the North/South Ministerial Council in Armagh

INWMG and Kilmainham / Inchicore events

2000 – INWMG included in Dublin City Council Record of Protected Structures
 – Herbaceous borders replanted inside yew hedges
2001 – Bookcases upgraded in book rooms at the INWMG
2004 – Viking objects discovered by a contractor while laying electrical cables at the garden of the Islandbridge lodge
2005 – Digitisation of the War Memorial Books
2006 – President McAleese, Taoiseach Bertie Ahern and members of Government commemorate the 90th anniversary of the Battle of the Somme
 – Closure of Christian Brothers School at Richmond Barracks
2008 – Archaeological excavations at the INWMG uncover a grave containing a sword, spearhead, and ringed pin

2011 – President McAleese and Queen Elizabeth II attend wreath-laying ceremony at the INWMG
2012 – Lord Mayors of Belfast and Dublin attend commemorations at the INWMG
2013 – Demolition of the last remaining block of St Michael's Estate, Inchicore
2014 – War Memorial Books now searchable online in a collaboration between Google, the In Flanders' Fields Museum (in Ypres, Belgium), and the Dept of Foreign Affairs and Trade
2015 – Conservation work of *Ireland's Memorial Records* completed by Marsh's Library, Dublin
 – Over 75 species of bumble bees recorded at the INWMG
 – OPW launches website for the INWMG (www.opwdublincommemorative.ie)

2016 – 100th anniversary of the Battle of the Somme at the INWMG, attended by President Michael D Higgins, Taoiseach Enda Kenny, NI Secretary Theresa Villiers and NI Deputy First Minister Martin McGuinness
 – OPW publishes its 'Irish National War Memorial Gardens Conservation Management Plan' (consultation draft)
2017 – Former Taoiseach, Liam Cosgrave, buried at Goldenbridge Cemetery, Inchicore, alongside his father WT Cosgrave, former President of Executive Council
2018 – 100th anniversary commemoration of armistice of World War I, 11th November
2019 – OPW commemorates 150th anniversary of the birth of Edwin Lutyens with an international architectural competition for a bridge across the River Liffey

2000s	**Decade of Centenaries 2012-23**	**Decade of Centenaries 2012-23**

Related Irish / UK events

2000 – Devolution suspended and returned to Northern Ireland
 – US President Clinton visits Ireland
2001 – Foot and mouth disease in UK and Ireland
 – 9/11 terrorist attacks in New York and Washington DC
 – PSNI established in Northern Ireland
2002 – Euro currency introduced
 – Treaty of Nice accepted in referendum
2003 – US/UK invasion of Iraq
2004 – Ireland holds Presidency of Council of EU
 – 10 new member states join EU
 – Guildford 4 and Maguire 7 exonerated by British Prime Minster, Tony Blair
2005 – Irish language granted official status in EU
 – Death of Pope John Paul II
2006 – International School for Peace Studies at Messines opens
 – Northern Ireland Assembly recalled
 – 90th anniversary of Easter Rising
2007 – Democratic Unionist Party attends North/South Ministerial Council Meeting
2008 – International financial crisis following global stock market downturn
2009 – Unemployment in Ireland reaches 9.2%

2010 – Saville Report into Bloody Sunday exonerates victims; apology issued by British Prime Minister, David Cameron
2011 – US President Barack Obama visits Ireland
 – Michael D Higgins inaugurated as 9th President of Ireland
2012 – President Higgins makes two official visits to London
 – Centenary of the Ulster Covenant
 – Centenary of Home Rule crisis
2013 – Centenary of the foundation of the Irish Volunteers
 – Centenary of the Dublin lock-out, the most severe industrial dispute in Irish history
2014 – Centenary of the start of World War I
 – First state visit by an Irish President to the UK
2015 – Centenary of the Gallipoli landings
 – Prince of Wales visits Mullaghmore, Co Sligo, where his great-uncle, Lord Mountbatten, was murdered by the IRA in 1979

2016 – Centenary of Easter Rising
 – Centenary of the Somme offensive
 – UK votes to leave the European Union in Brexit referendum
2018 – Centenary of the first sitting of the Dáil
 – Centenary of the introduction of women's suffrage
 – Centenary of the ending of World War I
2020 – Britain officially leaves the European Union
 – Global Covid-19 pandemic causes severe disruption and more than three million deaths worldwide

Drawings for the Irish National War Memorial

SIR EDWIN LUTYENS

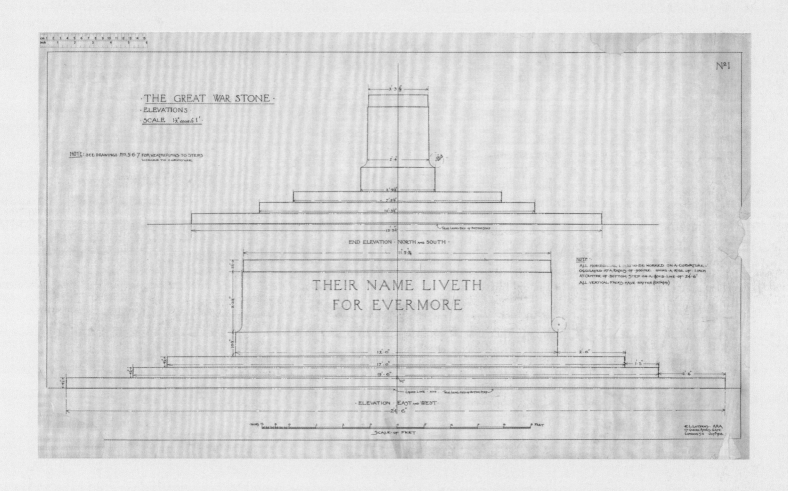

IRISH NATIONAL WAR MEMORIAL

⅛" SCALE SECTIONS — REFER TO DRAWING Nº 13.

NOTE — FOUNDATIONS TO BE MODIFIED AS NECESSARY TO SUIT SITE.

NOTE — DIMENSIONS IN RED ARE REVISIONS SUGGESTED BY
DATA SENT WITH LETTED DATED 27ᵀᴴ MARCH 1934, FROM
THE OFFICE OF PUBLIC WORKS, DUBLIN

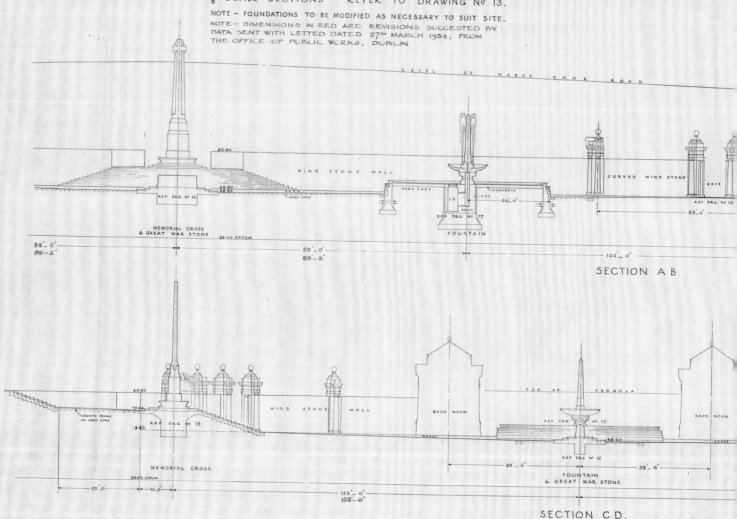

LEVEL OF HORSE SHOE ROAD

MEMORIAL CROSS
& GREAT WAR STONE

FOUNTAIN

CURVED WIND STONE GATE

WIND STONE WALL

SECTION A.B.

MEMORIAL CROSS

WIND STONE WALL

BOOK ROOM

TOP OF PERGOLA

BOOK ROOM

FOUNTAIN
& GREAT WAR STONE

SECTION C.D.

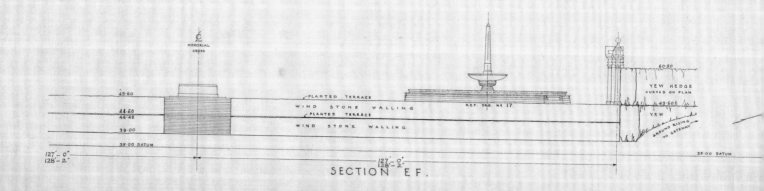

MEMORIAL
CROSS

PLANTED TERRACE

WIND STONE WALLING

PLANTED TERRACE

WIND STONE WALLING

YEW HEDGE
CURVED ON PLAN

YEW

GROUND RISING
TO GATEWAY

SECTION E.F.

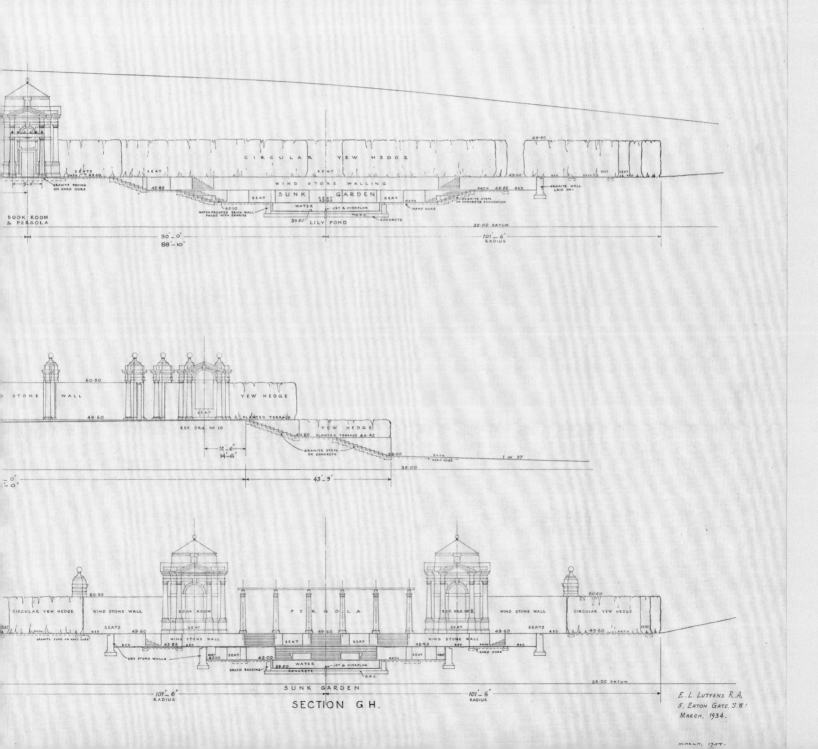

SECTION G.H.

SUNK GARDEN

E.L. Lutyens R.A.
5, Eaton Gate, S.W.1
March, 1934.

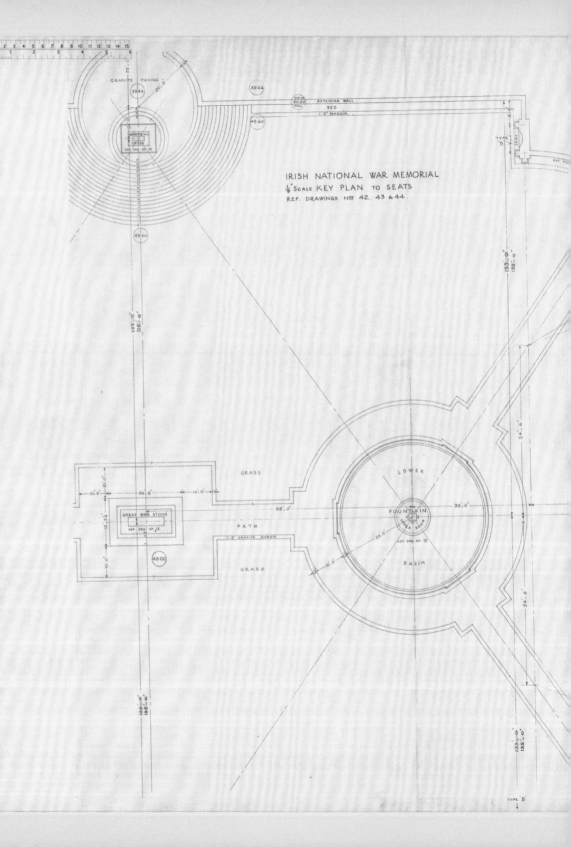

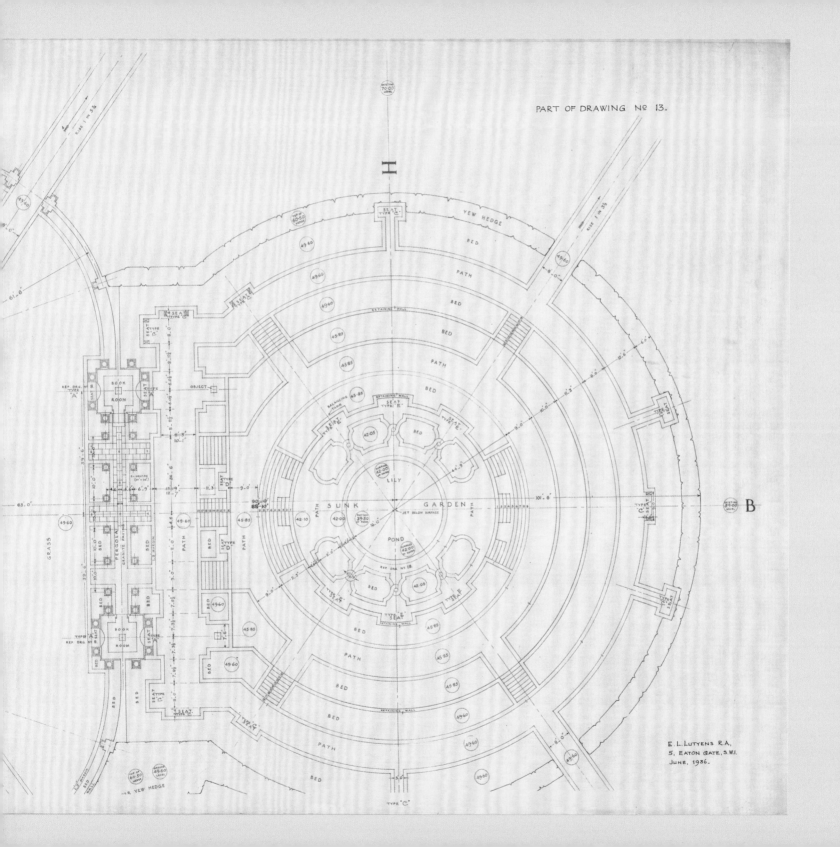

YEW HEDGE

BED

PATH

BED

BED

PATH

BED

SEAT TYPE "C"

SEAT TYPE "D"

BOOK ROOM

PERGOLA

GRANITE PAVING

OBJECT

SEAT TYPE "A"

REF. DRG. Nº B TYPE "A"

BED

BED

SEAT TYPE "D"

BED

LILY

POND

PATH   SUNK   GARDEN   PATH

JET BELOW SURFACE

BED

BED

BED

BED

BOOK ROOM

SEAT TYPE "A"

GRASS

BED

BED

TYPE "C" SEAT

BED

BED

PATH

BED

BED

RETAINING WALL

PATH

LOWER YEW HEDGE

TYPE "C"

E. L. LUTYENS R.A,
5, EATON GATE, S.W.I.
JUNE, 1936.

B

IRISH NATIONAL WAR MEMORIAL. DETAILS OF BOOK-ROOMS. SCALE ½ INCH EQUALS 1 FOOT.

AMENDING DRAWING Nº 8.

⅛" HAS BEEN ALLOWED FOR THICKNESS OF JOINTS IN MASONRY.

BUT FIGURED DIMENSIONS TO BE WORKED TO.

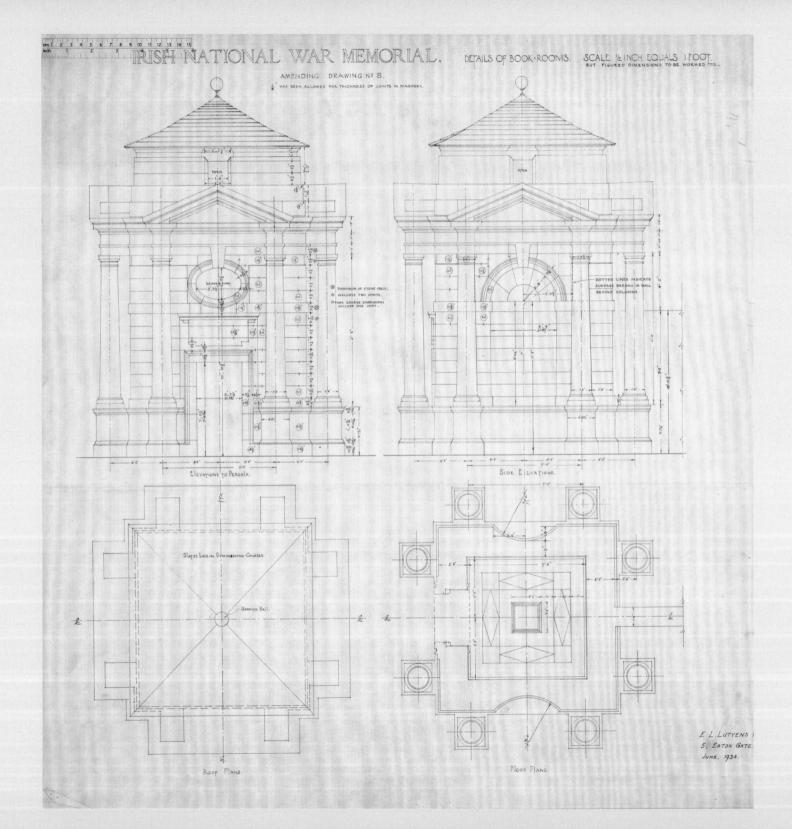

⊗ DIMENSION OF STONE ONLY.
⊕ INCLUDES TWO JOINTS.
OTHER COURSE DIMENSIONS
INCLUDE ONE JOINT.

ELEVATIONS TO PERGOLA.

DOTTED LINES INDICATE
SURFACE BREAKS IN WALL
BEHIND COLUMNS.

SIDE ELEVATIONS.

SLATES LAID IN DIMINISHING COURSES.

GRANITE BALL.

ROOF PLAN.

FLOOR PLAN.

E. L. LUTYENS
5, EATON GATE.
JUNE, 1934.

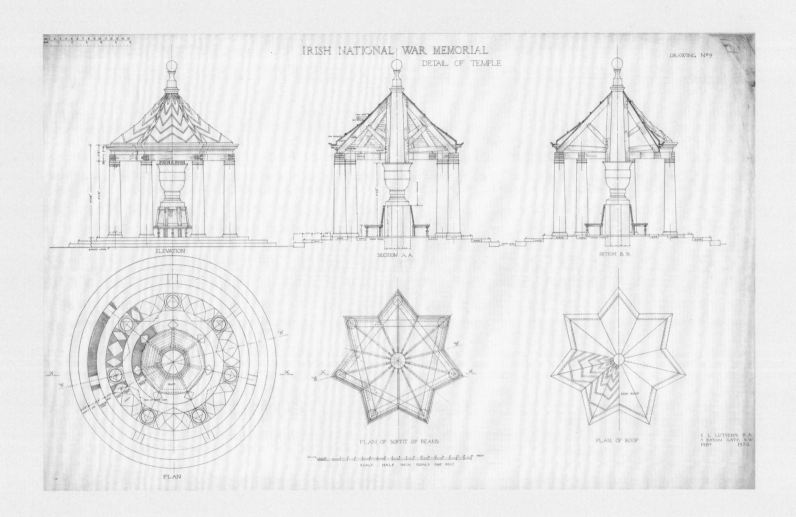

IRISH NATIONAL WAR MEMORIAL
DETAIL OF TEMPLE

DRAWING Nº 9

ELEVATION

SECTION A.A.

SETION B.B.

PLAN

PLAN OF SOFFIT OF BEAMS

PLAN OF ROOF

SCALE HALF INCH EQUALS ONE FOOT

E. L. LUTYENS R.A
5 EATON GATE S.W.
FEBY 1932

Irish National War Memorial
by Edwin Lutyens

(all drawings: OPW Library)

opposite

'Details of Book Rooms', 1934
(elevation to pergola, side elevation, roof plan and
floor plan)

above

'Detail of Temple' (unbuilt), 1932
(sections and elevations of temple intended for the
junction of the main axis and Chord Road)

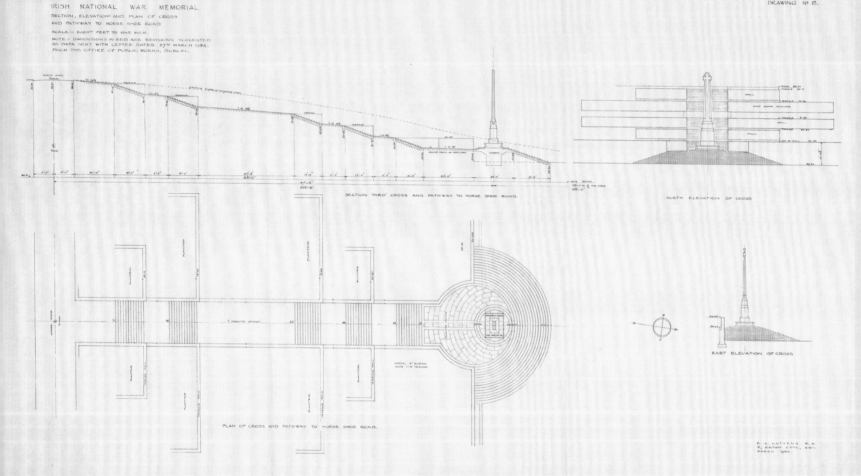

Irish National War Memorial
by Edwin Lutyens

(all drawings: OPW Library)

above

'Section, elevations and plan of Cross and
pathway to Horse Shoe Road', 1934

opposite

'Detail of Stone Cross (granite), 1934
(front and side elevations, sections and half-plans at upper
and base levels)

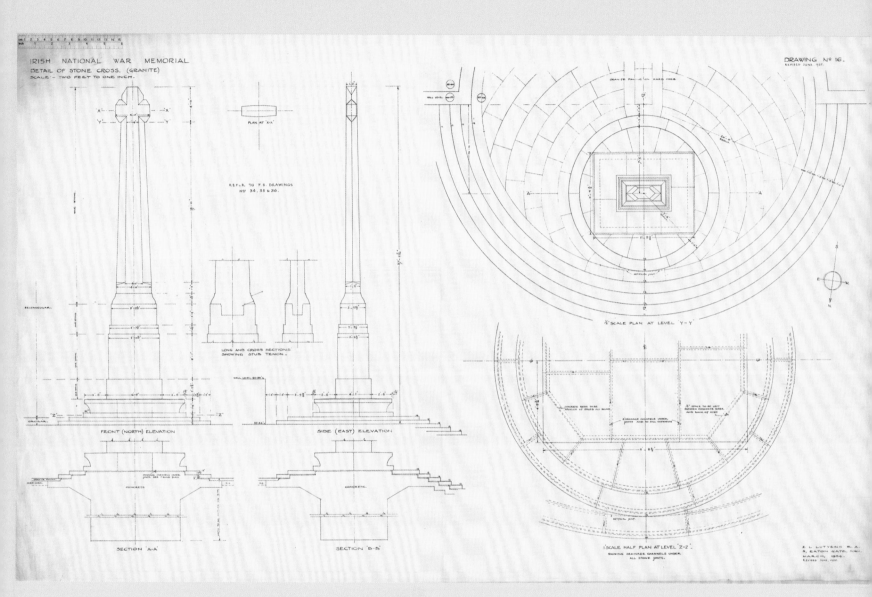

IRISH NATIONAL WAR MEMORIAL
DETAIL OF STONE CROSS. (GRANITE)
SCALE :- TWO FEET TO ONE INCH.

DRAWING Nº 16.
REVISED JUNE 1938.

PLAN AT X-X

REFER TO F.B. DRAWINGS
Nºs 34, 35 & 36.

LONG AND CROSS SECTIONS
SHOWING STUB TENON.

FRONT (NORTH) ELEVATION

SIDE (EAST) ELEVATION

SECTION 'A-A'

SECTION 'B-B'

½ SCALE PLAN AT LEVEL 'Y - Y'

1" SCALE HALF PLAN AT LEVEL 'Z-Z'
SHOWING DRAINAGE CHANNELS UNDER
ALL STONE JOINTS.

E. L. LUTYENS R. A.
5, EATON GATE, S.W.I.
MARCH, 1938.
REVISED JUNE 1938.

141

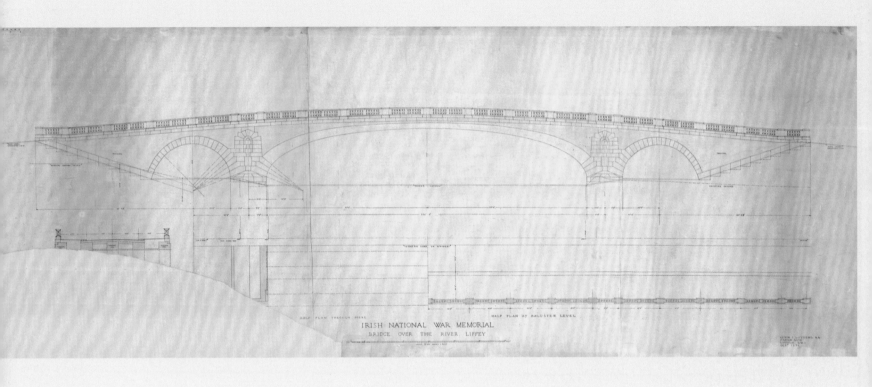

IRISH NATIONAL WAR MEMORIAL
BRIDGE OVER THE RIVER LIFFEY

Irish National War Memorial
by Edwin Lutyens

(all drawings: OPW Library)

'Bridge over the River Liffey', 1936
(elevation and half-plans through piers and at
baluster level)

opposite

'Outdoor seats in teak and granite', 1936
(plans, sections and elevations of 5 seat types, making up
50 seats in all)

page 144

'Detail of Fountain west of Great War Stone',
1934
(plans, sections and elevation)

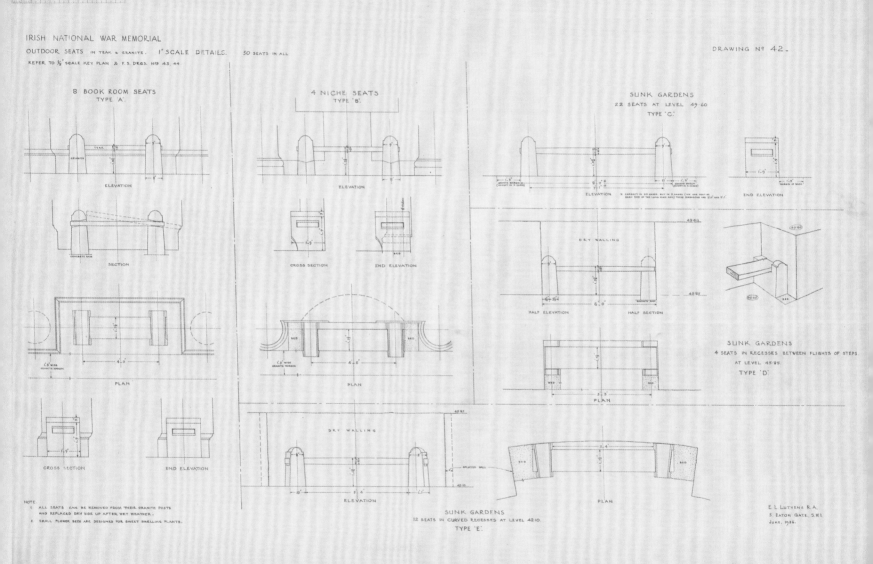

IRISH NATIONAL WAR MEMORIAL

OUTDOOR SEATS IN TEAK & GRANITE.   1" SCALE DETAILS.   50 SEATS IN ALL

REFER TO ⅛" SCALE KEY PLAN & F.S. DRGS. Nº§ 43. 44

8 BOOK ROOM SEATS
TYPE 'A'.

ELEVATION

SECTION

PLAN

CROSS SECTION   END ELEVATION

4 NICHE SEATS
TYPE 'B'.

ELEVATION

CROSS SECTION   END ELEVATION

PLAN

SUNK GARDENS
22 SEATS AT LEVEL 49·60
TYPE 'C'.

ELEVATION   END ELEVATION

DRY WALLING

HALF ELEVATION   HALF SECTION

PLAN

SUNK GARDENS
4 SEATS IN RECESSES BETWEEN FLIGHTS OF STEPS.
AT LEVEL 45·85.
TYPE 'D'.

PLAN

SUNK GARDENS
12 SEATS IN CURVED RECESSES AT LEVEL 42·10.
TYPE 'E'.

DRY WALLING

ELEVATION   PLAN

NOTE.
1. ALL SEATS CAN BE REMOVED FROM THEIR GRANITE POSTS
   AND REPLACED DRY SIDE UP AFTER WET WEATHER.
2. SMALL FLOWER BEDS ARE DESIGNED FOR SWEET SMELLING PLANTS.

E L LUTYENS R.A.
5. EATON GATE. S.W.I
JUNE. 1936.

IRISH NATIONAL WAR MEMORIAL

DETAIL OF FOUNTAIN WEST OF GREAT WAR STONE.
MATERIAL: GRANITE.
SCALE: TWO FEET TO ONE INCH
REFER TO DRGS NOS 13 AND 14.

DRAWING No 17

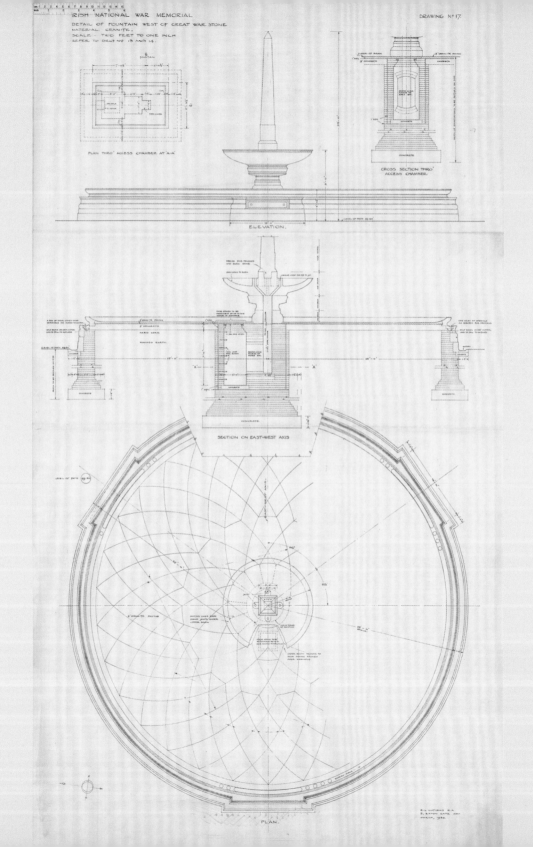

PLAN THRO' ACCESS CHAMBER AT 'A-A'

CROSS SECTION THRO'
ACCESS CHAMBER.

ELEVATION.

SECTION ON EAST-WEST AXIS

PLAN.

144